Arctic Imperative
Reinforcing U.S. Strategy on America's Fourth Coast

COUNCIL *on*
FOREIGN
RELATIONS

Independent Task Force Report No. 75

Thad W. Allen and
Christine Todd Whitman, *Chairs*
Esther Brimmer, *Project Director*

Arctic Imperatives

Reinforcing U.S. Strategy on America's Fourth Coast

The Council on Foreign Relations (CFR) is an independent, nonpartisan membership organization, think tank, and publisher dedicated to being a resource for its members, government officials, business executives, journalists, educators and students, civic and religious leaders, and other interested citizens in order to help them better understand the world and the foreign policy choices facing the United States and other countries. Founded in 1921, CFR carries out its mission by maintaining a diverse membership, with special programs to promote interest and develop expertise in the next generation of foreign policy leaders; convening meetings at its headquarters in New York and in Washington, DC, and other cities where senior government officials, members of Congress, global leaders, and prominent thinkers come together with CFR members to discuss and debate major international issues; supporting a Studies Program that fosters independent research, enabling CFR scholars to produce articles, reports, and books and hold roundtables that analyze foreign policy issues and make concrete policy recommendations; publishing *Foreign Affairs*, the preeminent journal on international affairs and U.S. foreign policy; sponsoring Independent Task Forces that produce reports with both findings and policy prescriptions on the most important foreign policy topics; and providing up-to-date information and analysis about world events and American foreign policy on its website, www.cfr.org.

The Council on Foreign Relations takes no institutional positions on policy issues and has no affiliation with the U.S. government. All views expressed in its publications and on its website are the sole responsibility of the author or authors.

The Council on Foreign Relations sponsors Independent Task Forces to assess issues of current and critical importance to U.S. foreign policy and provide policymakers with concrete judgments and recommendations. Diverse in backgrounds and perspectives, Task Force members aim to reach a meaningful consensus on policy through private deliberations. Once launched, Task Forces are independent of CFR and solely responsible for the content of their reports. Task Force members are asked to join a consensus signifying that they endorse "the general policy thrust and judgments reached by the group, though not necessarily every finding and recommendation." Each Task Force member also has the option of putting forward an additional or dissenting view. Members' affiliations are listed for identification purposes only and do not imply institutional endorsement. Task Force observers participate in discussions, but are not asked to join the consensus.

For further information about CFR or this Task Force, please write to the Council on Foreign Relations, 58 East 68th Street, New York, NY 10065, or call the Communications office at 212.434.9888. Visit CFR's website at www.cfr.org.

This report is printed on paper that is FSC® Chain-of-Custody Certified by a printer who is certified by BM TRADA North America Inc.

Task Force Members

Task Force members are asked to join a consensus signifying that they endorse "the general policy thrust and judgments reached by the group, though not necessarily every finding and recommendation." They participate in the Task Force in their individual, not institutional, capacities.

Thad W. Allen
Booz Allen Hamilton, Inc.

Scott G. Borgerson
CargoMetrics Technologies

Lawson W. Brigham*
University of Alaska Fairbanks

Esther Brimmer
NAFSA: Association of International Educators

Stephen A. Cheney
American Security Project

Charles F. Doran*
School of Advanced International Studies, Johns Hopkins University

Dalee Sambo Dorough*
University of Alaska Anchorage

Jill M. Dougherty*
Woodrow Wilson International Center for Scholars

Richard H. Fontaine Jr.*
Center for a New American Security

Sherri W. Goodman*
Woodrow Wilson International Center for Scholars

Katherine A. Hardin
IHS Markit

Jane Lubchenco
Oregon State University

Kimberly Marten
Barnard College, Columbia University

Marvin E. Odum

Sean Parnell*
Law Offices of Sean Parnell

James B. Steinberg
Maxwell School, Syracuse University

*The individual has endorsed the report and signed an additional or dissenting view.

Rockford Weitz
Fletcher School,
Tufts University

Christine Todd Whitman
Whitman Strategy Group, LLC

Margaret D. Williams
World Wildlife Fund

Kenneth S. Yalowitz
Woodrow Wilson International
Center for Scholars

Contents

Foreword

The Arctic is changing and may be ice free for periods of time in the near future, offering both opportunities and challenges for the United States and other Arctic countries. The Arctic is warming at double the rate of the rest of the world and the melting sea ice is opening new routes for ships, allowing access to valuable natural resources. Today, Arctic and non-Arctic countries alike are vying to take advantage of newfound possibilities, while also grappling with the effects of the changing landscape.

As the rotating chair of the Arctic Council—the international group created to promote the region's peaceful and responsible development—the United States has focused its Arctic policies on scientific cooperation, environmental conservation, and the protection of indigenous communities. Now, with the advent of a new administration and Congress, the United States should reevaluate the region's geopolitical importance, assess the competition from Russia and China, take measures to safeguard U.S. strategic interests, and explore greater economic development in the region.

Despite the increasing maritime activity in the Arctic, the United States lags behind others in its capabilities. The United States possesses only two functional icebreaking ships that serve both the Arctic and Antarctic. This shortcoming limits the United States' ability to maneuver in icy waters and defend its interests in the region. The melting polar ice cap is exposing the region's economic potential, providing access to hydrocarbons and minerals beneath the ice, and creating new commercial opportunities that the United States has been slow to pursue. Alaska, America's Arctic, does not have adequate deepwater ports, roads, or even reliable internet access; it needs greater investment in infrastructure to support its economic development. Moreover, what happens in the Arctic has global repercussions. Rising sea levels, coastal erosion, and changing migration patterns affect far-flung areas and require attention and planning.

The Council on Foreign Relations (CFR) convened an Independent Task Force to examine current U.S. strategy toward the Arctic amidst the region's unprecedented transformation. The Task Force recommends several changes to U.S. policy to better protect and promote growing U.S. economic and strategic interests.

First, the report makes a strong case for ratification of the UN Convention on the Law of the Sea in order to secure U.S. rights to resources on Alaska's extended continental shelf. The report also advocates for funding and building additional icebreakers to improve operational capacity in the region. It proposes greater investment in telecommunications, energy, roads, and other infrastructure to support the economic development of the American Arctic. Building on the work of the Arctic Council, the Task Force recommends strengthening international cooperation on security issues with all Arctic states, including Russia. Finally, the Task Force urges consultation with Alaska Natives to ensure that development in the region benefits the well-being of those who live there.

I would like to thank Task Force chairs Thad Allen and Christine Todd Whitman for their leadership, expertise, and dedication to this project. I also wish to recognize the individual Task Force members and observers, whose knowledge and experience helped produce a useful report. I am grateful to Anya Schmemann, director of CFR's Independent Task Force Program, for successfully guiding this project from its inception. Finally, I extend my thanks to Project Director Esther Brimmer for taking on this multifaceted issue and working closely with Task Force members to produce a document that reflects the Arctic's enhanced importance and underscores the need for the United States to adjust its policies and capabilities consistent with this reality.

Richard N. Haass
President
Council on Foreign Relations
March 2017

Acknowledgments

The Arctic is known as a remote and frozen region, but rapidly changing conditions there are opening up the previously inaccessible area to new opportunities—and new dangers. This Council-sponsored Independent Task Force report, *Arctic Imperatives: Reinforcing U.S. Strategy on America's Fourth Coast,* is the product of much work and effort by the dedicated members and observers of the Independent Task Force on U.S. Strategy in the Arctic. It was a pleasure to work with and learn from such a knowledgeable and varied group of individuals, and I am deeply appreciative of the guidance and extensive feedback they contributed over the course of this project.

In particular, I would like to thank our distinguished co-chairs, Admiral Thad Allen and Governor Christine Todd Whitman, who were instrumental in leading this Task Force. It was a privilege to have worked closely with them over the past year.

My gratitude extends to several individuals who lent their advice and expertise to this project. Of course, none of them bears responsibility for the ultimate content of this report. Mark Brzezinski, who recently served as executive director of the White House's Arctic Executive Steering Committee, briefed the Task Force at its outset and was a helpful resource throughout. I also thank the members of the Alaska congressional delegation—Senators Lisa Murkowski and Dan Sullivan and Representative Don Young—for sharing their perspectives on Arctic and Alaska issues. The report also benefited from individual consultations with a number of officials, including at the U.S. Departments of State and Defense, the embassies of Canada and Finland, and the U.S. Arctic Research Commission. In addition, the report benefited from the expertise and advice of Marcus D. King and Marlene Laruelle of George Washington University.

The conclusions of this report were greatly informed by the Task Force's research trip to Alaska in August 2016, led by co-chairs Thad and Christie. Our meetings with experts and community leaders in Anchorage, Nome, and Kotzebue offered a valuable range of perspectives that helped to shape this final report. I am grateful to the many individuals who shared their insights and expertise with our Task Force delegation, including those from the Alaska Center; Alaska Department of Commerce, Community, and Economic Development; Alaska Department of Environmental Conservation; Alaska Ocean Observing System; Alaska Oil and Gas Association; Alaska Wilderness League; Alaskan Command (ALCOM); Aleutian and Bering Sea Islands Landscape Conservation Cooperative; Alyeska Pipeline Service Company; Anchorage Economic Development Corporation; Arctic Economic Council (Alaska delegation); Arctic Slope Regional Corporation; Audubon Alaska; Bering Straits Native Corporation; Bureau of Ocean Energy Management; City of Nome; Inuit Circumpolar Council-Alaska; Kawerak, Inc.; Maniilaq Association; Marine Advisory Program; NANA Regional Corporation; National Weather Service; North Pacific Research Board; Pacific Environment; Renewable Energy Alaska Project; University of Alaska, Anchorage; University of Alaska, Fairbanks; U.S. Arctic Research Commission; U.S. Coast Guard; Western Alaska Landscape Conservation Cooperative; Wilderness Society; and World Wildlife Fund. The Task Force delegation also benefited from the knowledge and hospitality of Alice Rogoff and Reggie Joule during our trip. Special thanks to the personnel at Joint Base Elmendorf-Richardson for facilitating our base visit and briefings with ALCOM and U.S. Coast Guard officials.

I extend thanks to CFR's outstanding staff who made producing this report a pleasure. I would like to thank CFR's Publications team for their work in editing and readying the report for publication. CFR's Communications, Corporate, Digital, Meetings, National, Outreach, and Washington Program teams all have worked to ensure the report reaches the widest audience possible, and I am appreciative of their efforts.

CFR Task Force Program Director Anya Schmemann was integral to this project from start to finish, and I am grateful for her guidance and support throughout the process. Veronica Chiu and Chelie Setzer of the Task Force Program deserve credit for their diligent work in ensuring the Task Force ran smoothly, from organizing each meeting, to arranging our trip to Alaska, to editing multiple drafts of the report and preparing it for release. Research Associate Theresa Lou and intern Rebecca Hunziker provided valuable research assistance during the drafting process as well. I am also thankful to Holly Rogers and Jennifer Hopkins in the co-chairs' offices for their assistance throughout this project.

Finally, I am grateful to CFR President Richard N. Haass for giving me the opportunity to direct this important effort and for identifying the Arctic as a region of concern and interest.

Esther Brimmer
Project Director

Acronyms

AESC	Arctic Executive Steering Committee
ARPA	Arctic Research and Policy Act
ASEAN	Association of South East Asian Nations
DEW	Distant Early Warning
ECS	extended continental shelf
EEZ	exclusive economic zone
EUCOM	European Command
°F	degree Fahrenheit
FY	fiscal year
GDP	gross domestic product
GIPPS	Global Integrated Polar Prediction System
GPS	Global Positioning System
IMO	International Maritime Organization
NASA	National Aeronautics and Space Administration
NATO	North Atlantic Treaty Organization
NOAA	National Oceanic and Atmospheric Administration
NORAD	North American Aerospace Defense
NORTHCOM	Northern Command
NSF	National Science Foundation
OSCE	Organization for Security and Cooperation in Europe
PACOM	Pacific Command
QZSS	Quasi-Zenith Satellite System
SBAS	satellite-based augmentation system

TAPS	Trans Alaska Pipeline System
UCP	unified command plan
UNCLOS	UN Convention on the Law of the Sea
VHF	very high frequency
WMO	World Meteorological Organization

Independent Task Force Report

MAP 1: MAP OF THE ARCTIC

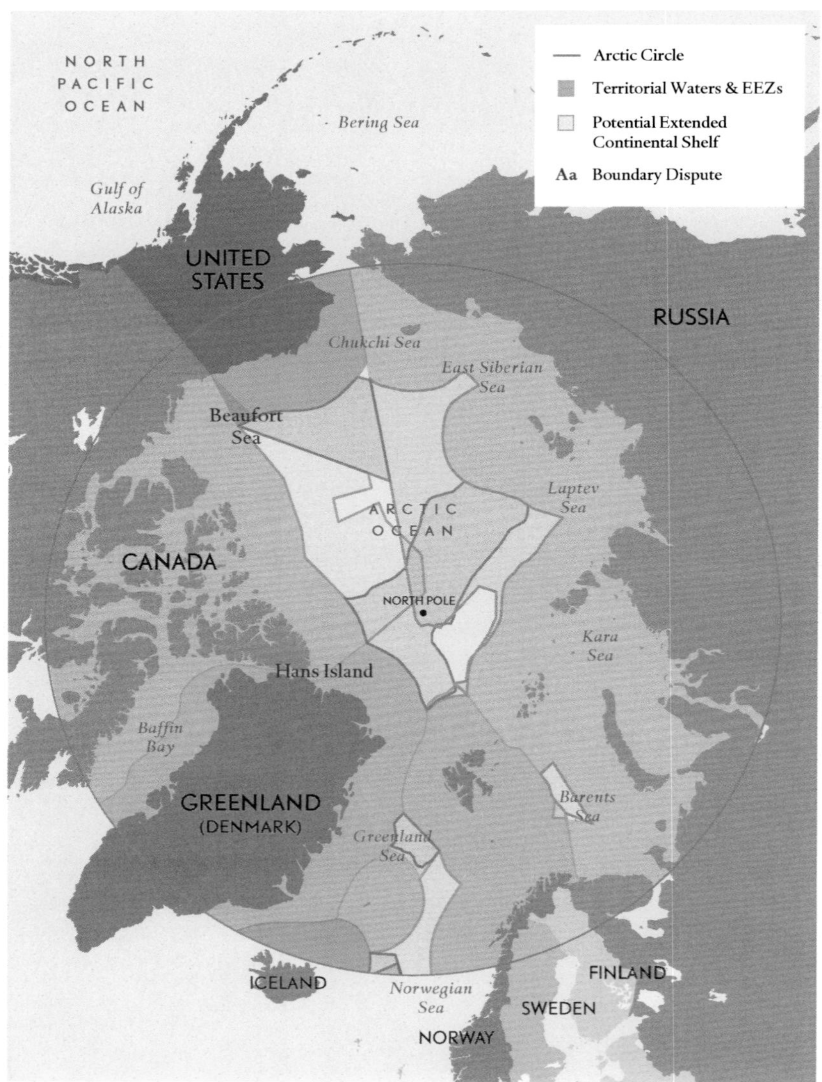

Introduction

The Arctic is a crossroads of international politics and a forewarning for the world. The United States, through Alaska, is a significant Arctic nation with strategic, economic, and scientific interests. As sea ice continues to melt, countries inside and outside the Arctic region have updated their strategic and commercial calculations to take advantage of the changing conditions stemming from the opening of the region. The United States needs to increase its strategic commitment to the region or risk leaving its interests unprotected.

The rate of warming in the Arctic region is significantly faster than scientists expected—almost twice that of the rest of the world—and is opening the once-inaccessible region to commerce, transport, resource extraction, and numerous benefits and ills. The warming in the Arctic also affects far-flung areas; Arctic ice loss and melting of the Greenland ice sheet raise sea levels and threaten coastal communities around the globe. The thawing permafrost also releases carbon and methane, which in turn contribute to the rise in global temperature.

Against this backdrop, the United States is chairing the Arctic Council—the intergovernmental forum that addresses issues related to the Arctic—from 2015 to 2017, allowing U.S. policymakers to set the agenda for regional cooperation and advance U.S. interests in the region. The opening of the Arctic offers economic and commercial opportunities, such as new shipping routes and potentially sizeable oil and gas resources, but also exposes local populations and ecosystems to climate-related risks. At the same time, an increased presence and pace of activities by Russia and growing interest from China raise concerns for the United States and other Arctic nations about Russian and Chinese intentions.

To complement its long-term, integrated strategies across the Atlantic, Asia Pacific, and Western Hemisphere, the United States should commit to a more comprehensive approach to the Arctic, which is effectively its fourth sea coast. As security concerns diminished after the end of the Cold War, U.S. Arctic policy focused on scientific, energy, and environmental issues. These topics remain important, but increased activity by other countries necessitates a more strategic approach to U.S. policy in the region while continuing to uphold the cooperative vision of the Arctic Council.

The Council on Foreign Relations convened this Independent Task Force to assess challenges and opportunities for the United States in the Arctic region in the face of changing conditions there. The Task Force finds that the Arctic is of growing economic and geostrategic importance and seeks to highlight specific actions U.S. officials should take to improve the United States' strategic presence in the Arctic region.

The Task Force has identified six main goals for the United States in the Arctic:

- securing U.S. rights to perhaps more than 386,000 square miles (1 million square kilometers) of subsea resources on the extended continental shelf by ratifying the UN Convention on the Law of the Sea (UNCLOS)
- funding up to six icebreakers operated by the U.S. Coast Guard and having at least three operational in the polar regions at any one time
- improving telecommunications, energy, and other infrastructure in Alaska to support a sustained security presence and economic diversification
- deepening work with all Arctic states, including Russia, on confidence-building and cooperative security measures through the Arctic Council
- supporting sustainable development for the people of the Arctic and further consulting with Alaska Natives to improve their well-being
- sustaining robust research funding to understand the ongoing profound changes in the region and their impact on the globe

The United States needs to bolster its infrastructure and assets in the Arctic to safeguard its strategic interests, defend its national borders, protect the environment, and maintain its scientific and technological leadership.

The Arctic Region

The Arctic region is warming at twice the rate as the rest of the planet, and the Arctic Ocean now experiences longer periods of open water and more activity than ever before in human history, which presents new opportunities as well as new risks. By some estimates, the region will be ice free for one month each year by 2040—an extraordinary development. As the ice melts, the Arctic is changing, opening up new shipping routes and opportunities to reach valuable resources on and below the seabed. Rising sea levels, softening coastline ice, and warmer temperatures are already changing the way people live and work in the region. In November 2016, during the season when polar night descends and the sun barely shines, the daily average temperature in the Arctic was a remarkable 36°F warmer than usual. Sea ice cover that month was less than the previous low level in November 2012.[1] What happens in the Arctic does not stay in the Arctic. Indeed, the challenge in the Arctic foreshadows the looming challenge elsewhere.

Definitions of the Arctic vary.[2] The Arctic Council member states are defined by their geography, either on or above the Arctic Circle, at a latitude of approximately 66° 33' north of the equator. Under the Arctic Research and Policy Act (ARPA) of 1984, the U.S. government defines the Arctic region as "all U.S. and foreign territory north of the Arctic Circle and all U.S. territory north and west of the boundary formed by the Porcupine, Yukon, and Kuskokwim Rivers, and all contiguous areas and straits north of and adjacent to the Arctic Circle."[3] This report uses the more expansive definition to facilitate consideration of issues that span Arctic and subarctic areas.

The coastal geography throughout the Arctic varies significantly. The Nordic countries have rocky coastlines with deepwater areas. These Nordic regions, along with northwest Russia and the Kola Peninsula, are ice free. Russia has the longest Arctic coast, at nearly twenty-five thousand miles.[4] Along the Arctic Ocean coast, Alaska, the northernmost U.S. state, features lagoons, bays, wetlands, river deltas, and a major coastal plain; and Canada's Arctic includes numerous lightly populated, high Arctic islands.

The Arctic Ocean sea ice cover is melting faster than predicted. Whereas sea ice, defined as "frozen ocean water," can reflect up to 80 percent of the sunlight that falls on it, dark open ocean water absorbs heat, speeding the melting process.[5] Each month, scientists check the minimum extent of sea ice, and satellites observed the lowest extent of Arctic sea ice ever recorded in September 2012 and the second lowest level in September 2016 (figure 1).[6] Recent analyses based on data collected since 1850 indicate no precedent for such low levels.[7] Some scientists predict that by the 2030s there could be virtually no sea ice cover for a time each summer, only exacerbating the problem.

Warming conditions are more pronounced in the Arctic than in lower latitudes (figure 2). Observers note that the average annual temperature in the Arctic region is 1.8°F warmer than was normal from 1961 to 1990. Temperatures from October to November have reached 9°F above the baseline.[8] The melting ice could displace local communities

*FIGURE 1: ANOMALIES IN ARCTIC SEA ICE EXTENT FROM 1981 TO 2016**

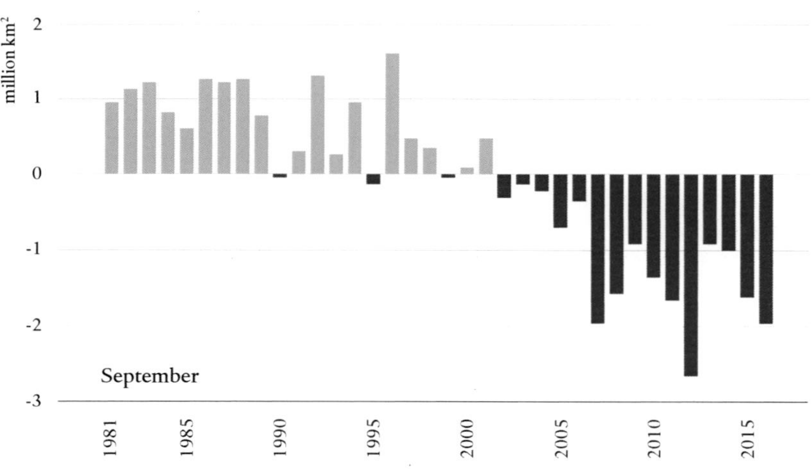

*Sea ice extent represents all areas with at least 15 percent ice concentration. This graph depicts the deviation from the mean sea ice extent for the years 1979–2015 for the month of September.

Source: F. Fetterer, K. Knowles, W. Meier, and M. Savoie, *Sea Ice Index, Version 2* (Boulder, CO: National Snow and Ice Data Center, 2016), https://nsidc.org/data/g02135#.

FIGURE 2: DIFFERENCE IN ARCTIC AND GLOBAL AVERAGE ANNUAL SURFACE AIR TEMPERATURE FROM 1900 TO 2016

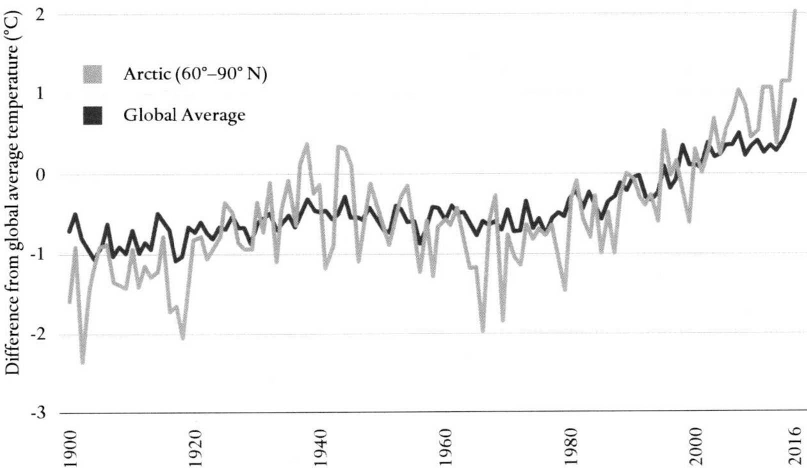

Source: J. Richter-Menge, J. E. Overland, and J. T. Mathis, eds., *Arctic Report Card 2016* (Washington, DC: National Oceanic and Atmospheric Administration, December 2016), ftp://ftp.oar.noaa.gov/arctic/documents/ArcticReportCard_full_report2016.pdf.

and military bases and limit the habitat of polar bears and other Arctic animals, affecting the lifestyle of those who depend on subsistence hunting and fishing throughout the region. Warmer temperatures are also thawing the permafrost. Structures built on permafrost, such as roads, are sagging. Storms and erosion eat away at coasts no longer protected by extensive sea ice. Melting of the Greenland ice cap alone could increase global sea levels significantly, possibly by an estimated twenty feet.[9]

These changes will have an especially significant impact on Alaska and Alaska Natives in that some communities may no longer be habitable and traditional ways of life may change. Thirty-one communities in Alaska are under threat from coastal erosion and twelve are already relocating.[10] It is too late for restoration of the coastline; the adaptation is to move.[11] Dilemmas visible in Alaska may also be harbingers of challenges to come. Four thousand miles away, at the opposite end of the country, Miami-Dade County in Florida estimates that its coastal waters will rise four to seven inches by 2030.[12] With shorelines on both the Atlantic Ocean and the Gulf of Mexico and billions of dollars' worth of coastal property, Florida is deeply affected by these changes.[13] Meanwhile, Norfolk, Virginia, home of the largest naval base in the world, already floods often, and the New York and New Jersey coastlines are projected to see at least one foot of sea level rise by 2050, possibly as soon as the 2030s.[14]

Although the United States has held Arctic territory since it purchased Alaska from the Russian Empire in 1867, the region has not been central to U.S. national identity. The frontier and the Wild West have been more potent images in the American story. By contrast, the Far North has shaped the national consciousness in Canada, Russia, and Nordic countries. The European Arctic regions also have more infrastructure and inhabitants; of the four million people who live in the Arctic, more than 70 percent are in Eurasia.[15] This is because some of the region is not considered an Arctic climate, but rather more temperate and ice free because of the warming effect of the Gulf Stream and North Atlantic Drift.

U.S. Policy

Over the past decade and across presidential administrations of both political parties, the United States has rekindled an interest in the Arctic as part of its national strategy, working to address scientific, technological, cultural, energy, and environmental issues in the region. Recent years have witnessed increased presidential attention to the Arctic, and the confluence of changing conditions and the U.S. chairmanship of the Arctic Council from 2015 to 2017 have occasioned a concerted effort to craft an ambitious U.S. policy.

Interest in the Arctic is and has been bipartisan. In January 2009, President George W. Bush issued an Arctic region policy just before leaving office. National Security Presidential Directive 66 (also known as Homeland Security Presidential Directive 25) declared an enduring theme: "The United States is an Arctic nation, with varied and compelling interests in that region."[16] In 2013, President Barack Obama issued a National Strategy for the Arctic Region, which elevated three goals for the United States: advancing U.S. security interests, pursuing responsible Arctic region stewardship, and strengthening international cooperation; it was followed by an implementation plan in 2014.[17]

The Arctic Council is an important venue for U.S. diplomacy. Chartered in 1996 as an intergovernmental forum, the Arctic Council is the leading organization in the region. Composed of eight Arctic countries—Canada, Denmark (Greenland), Finland, Iceland, Norway, Russia, Sweden, and the United States—the Arctic Council is a consultative body that operates by consensus.[18] In addition to the eight national governments, six indigenous groups are "permanent participants": the Aleut International Association, Arctic Athabaskan Council, Gwich'in Council International, Inuit Circumpolar Council, Russian Association of Indigenous Peoples of the North, and Saami Council. Included as the council's observers are twelve non-Arctic states, nine intergovernmental and interparliamentary organizations, and eleven nongovernmental organizations (NGOs).[19]

During its Arctic Council chairmanship from 2015 to 2017, the United States has been an active chair, giving higher political priority to this region than it had previously. Under the rubric "One Arctic: Shared Opportunities, Challenges and Responsibilities," the Obama administration outlined three priorities for U.S. chairmanship of the Arctic Council: "improving economic and living conditions in Arctic communities; Arctic Ocean safety, security and stewardship; and addressing the impacts of climate change."[20] The Task Force finds that these priorities are a good first step, but they should be sustained by the new administration of President Donald J. Trump if they are to have a lasting effect.

The United States can capitalize on strong relations with Canada and with the Nordic countries. The 2016 summit meeting between President Obama and Canadian Prime Minister Justin Trudeau resulted in the "U.S.-Canada Joint Statement on Climate, Energy, and Arctic Leadership," with cooperation in the Arctic embedded in this latest expression of U.S.-Canadian amity. New Arctic initiatives include partnering with indigenous peoples, setting aside wilderness space, and protecting fisheries.[21] The Task Force agrees that U.S.-Canada cooperation should include these areas in addition to national security. At the U.S.-Nordic Leaders Summit in May 2016, the United States and the five Nordic countries issued a joint statement affirming the importance of the region and their commitment to maintaining the Arctic as a "zone of peace and stability . . . based on universally recognized principles of international law including those reflected in the United Nations Convention on the Law of the Sea."[22] In December 2016, the United States and Canada jointly announced a ban on oil drilling in their neighboring Arctic waters.[23] The Task Force agrees with the U.S. State Department's International Security Advisory Board that Russia and other countries should be encouraged to associate with this agreement "to apply strict environmental standards and climate goals to commercial activities in the Arctic."[24]

The United States benefits from a rules-based international order that enhances economic well-being, respects human rights and human dignity, and supports mechanisms for the peaceful resolution of disputes while providing for territorial integrity and defense of the United States and its allies. In the Arctic, which is in rapid flux due to the changing climate, no one country can manage the coming challenges alone. A collective approach is needed to mitigate and adapt to changing realities, advance scientific understanding, and build resilience and capacity; the UN Convention on the Law of the Sea is part of this rule-based order.

LAW OF THE SEA

Under UNCLOS, the United States is entitled to an area twice the size of California—more than 386,000 square miles—of possibly resource-rich Arctic seabed along its extended continental shelf (ECS).[25] However, the United States is first required to ratify UNCLOS to secure its claim to the oil, gas, and other resources that may be present. Absence from this international mechanism impedes the ability of the United States to defend its legal claims to the Arctic seabed. Even though it is not eligible to submit its claim, the United States has been developing its case with the UN Commission on the Limits of the Continental Shelf. Although the United States is not a treaty party, U.S. military forces adhere to the tenets of UNCLOS because the treaty enhances U.S. assertion of freedom of navigation.

More than 160 countries have ratified the treaty, but the United States remains an outlier. The Bush and Obama administrations both supported approval of the convention, but opposition in the U.S. Senate remains. Opponents charge that UNCLOS accession is unnecessary for defending U.S. interests in the Arctic and would require the United States to cede sovereignty to an international body.[26] Yet without the treaty, the United States cannot claim and use resources beyond its two-hundred-nautical-mile exclusive economic zone (EEZ), and other countries could have their overlapping claims substantiated by the Commission on the Limits of the Continental Shelf (map 1).

Recognizing the political obstacles, the Task Force strongly urges the U.S. Senate to provide its advice and consent for the ratification of UNCLOS and recommends that the Trump administration make this a high priority for its work with the Senate. The Task Force finds that the convention would serve U.S. national security, economic, and environmental interests. It would also codify U.S. legal rights to exploit oil and gas resources on the ECS off the coast of Alaska, mine valuable minerals on the deep seabed, and lay and service submarine telecommunications cables. The United States should secure these resources to retain economic and strategic choices in the future. Even friendly neighbors are moving to claim these resources; the United States should not lose out.

U.S. GOVERNMENT

Under the Obama administration, Arctic policy was organized around scientific cooperation and adaptation to climate change rather than national security or economic analysis. Accordingly, the Arctic Executive Steering Committee (AESC) reports to the president via the Office of Science and Technology Policy, not the National Security Council or the National Economic Council. Further underscoring the Obama administration's emphasis on the importance of science in the region, the United States hosted the first Arctic Science Ministerial on September 28, 2016.

The Task Force supports the scientific focus of current U.S. Arctic policy. As a powerhouse in science and research, the United States plays to its strength by focusing in this area. Unlike the Eurasian and Nordic parts of the Arctic, the North American Arctic is lightly populated and unlikely to be a centerpiece of national economic growth. Moreover, scientific cooperation is relevant to many of the needs in the Arctic, including hydrography, telecommunications, and alternative energy. However, sustained budget support beyond fiscal year (FY) 2017 will be needed to realize initiatives launched by the Obama administration.

In addition to ongoing diplomatic efforts to conclude a binding agreement on scientific cooperation under the auspices of the Arctic Council, the United States could also explore new initiatives, such as ways to enforce the new International Maritime Organization (IMO) Polar Code safety requirements on vessels entering national ports or the creation of a multinational joint search and rescue operations center.

The Trump administration should consider how best to organize itself to manage Arctic issues after completion of the U.S. term as chair of the Arctic Council in May 2017. In 2014, the State Department created a new position of special representative for the Arctic. In 2015, the White House created the AESC, which coordinates six interagency working groups. These have been useful coordinating mechanisms and have helped prioritize Arctic issues in the federal government. In August 2015, Obama became the first U.S. president to travel to the

Arctic Circle while in office, helping shine a spotlight on the region. The Task Force recommends that the Trump administration maintain a White House–based coordination mechanism on Arctic issues. The work of many federal agencies affects the Arctic and can be counterproductive without explicit coordination. For instance, the Department of the Interior and the Environmental Protection Agency both regulate natural habitat in Alaska, and the Department of Commerce manages fisheries and houses the National Oceanic and Atmospheric Administration (NOAA). Both the State Department and the Department of Homeland Security, the parent agency of the U.S. Coast Guard, contribute to international cooperation in the Arctic.

The State Department's Arctic diplomatic work should be headed by an official with ambassadorial rank who would report to the assistant secretary for the Bureau of Oceans and International Environmental and Scientific Affairs. This option for an Arctic ambassador follows the model of other ambassadors. For example, the ambassador to the Association of South East Asian Nations (ASEAN) is part of the Bureau of East Asia and Pacific Affairs.

FINDINGS AND RECOMMENDATIONS FOR STRENGTHENING U.S. POLICY ON THE ARCTIC

The Task Force finds that

- by failing to ratify the UNCLOS treaty, the U.S. Senate has undermined the nation's ability to advance its interests in the Arctic to the fullest extent; and
- Arctic policies conducted by the major departments across the U.S. government need a formal coordination mechanism in the White House.

The Task Force recommends that

- the U.S. Senate provide its advice and consent on the ratification of UNCLOS to secure the country's legal rights to resources on the continental shelf;
- the United States continue its robust diplomacy in the Arctic Council

and maintain the council's focus on sustainable development, environmental protection, and continued involvement of the Arctic's indigenous peoples;

- U.S. policymakers better integrate and elevate Arctic issues in U.S. bilateral relations with Canada and with Nordic countries;
- the Trump administration maintain the role of the AESC as a White House–based coordination mechanism for the interagency process; and
- the Trump administration designate an Arctic ambassador reporting to the assistant secretary for the Bureau of Oceans and International Environmental and Scientific Affairs within the State Department. This ambassador could simultaneously serve as a deputy assistant secretary.

U.S. National Security

The United States needs to bolster its infrastructure and assets in the Arctic to safeguard its strategic interests, including defense of its national borders, the safety of Alaska, and relations with important countries such as Canada, China, and Russia. U.S. strategic choices guide its diplomacy in international organizations and its military deployments in the global commons, especially ocean navigation. The United States has a long-standing national security interest in the freedom of navigation and maritime domain control. The Task Force finds that a strengthened U.S. position in the Arctic—including increased presence, domain awareness, and capabilities—is an important national security imperative.

During the Cold War, the United States and Soviet Union watched each other across this region, and the United States, Canada, Denmark, and Iceland maintained a system of radar stations across the Arctic called the Distant Early Warning (DEW) Line. Today, Russia's actions in the Arctic require close scrutiny, and rising U.S.-Russia tensions in other regions may affect relations in the Arctic. In the early twenty-first century, though territorial defense remains important, U.S. security concerns have widened to include issues such as access to energy and environmental security.

Regardless of the mandate of the Arctic Council, which excludes military security, U.S. allied defense commitments include the Arctic. Five Arctic countries—Canada, Denmark, Iceland, Norway, and the United States—are North Atlantic Treaty Organization (NATO) allies; Finland and Sweden are partner countries but not formal allies. Norway leads the annual NATO Cold Response winter warfighting exercises, which in 2016 included twelve NATO members along with Finland and Sweden.[27] Although not a major issue at the 2016 NATO Summit, the Arctic, like the Atlantic Ocean and the Baltic and Mediterranean Seas, will certainly remain an area of interest for the alliance. The alliance commitments among the five Arctic states that are NATO members can have beneficial spillover into their preparedness in the Arctic. For example, as part of efforts to move closer to the alliance commitment of spending 2 percent of gross domestic product (GDP) on defense issues, Norway is bolstering its expenditures, including in Arctic defense.[28]

The Arctic region has enjoyed a refreshingly cooperative spirit largely insulated from political tensions in the rest of the world. However, disputes over Russian actions in Crimea, Ukraine, and elsewhere hover at the edge of Arctic amity. The United States has been concerned about Russian military activity in the region, and Russia has been alarmed by the expansion of NATO, the European Union's association agreement with Ukraine, and fears of a Western effort to gain control over Russia's resources.[29] The Trump administration has signaled a new, more transactional approach to Russia, and a lessening of tensions in other areas may help U.S.-Russia relations in the Arctic.

RUSSIA

The countries in the Arctic region remain at peace and cooperation among them is significant, especially on scientific and safety issues, but historical collaboration in the region is threatened by U.S.-Russia tensions elsewhere. The United States faces one of its most critical and difficult strategic challenges in interpreting Russia's intentions in the Arctic, and tensions from Russia's activities in Ukraine and other geopolitical contests have seeped into the region's politics. For instance, Russia no longer participates in the Arctic Security Forces Roundtable, a forum sponsored by the United States European Command (EUCOM). In addition, U.S. officials' participation in multilateral conferences with Russian counterparts now requires higher-level political approval. Nevertheless, Russia joined Canada, Denmark, Finland, and Norway in observing the U.S. Coast Guard and Northern Command (NORTHCOM) Arctic Chinook search and rescue simulation exercise in the summer of 2016.

Despite reemerging rivalries, collaboration in the Arctic recalls another extreme environment, outer space. Even with heightened tensions during the Cold War, the United States and the Soviet Union worked together in space and even concluded an agreement to rescue each other's astronauts. The Task Force finds that the same principles should apply in the Arctic.

For Russia, the Arctic is an important component of its economy. Before sanctions were imposed on Russia following its 2014 intervention in Ukraine, products from the Arctic Circle accounted for 20 percent of its GDP and 22 percent of its exports.[30] The Arctic remains central to Russia's strategy for economic growth because a large proportion of the next generation of oil and gas production is expected to come from Arctic development, both onshore and offshore. Ninety-five percent of Russia's natural gas and 75 percent of its oil is produced in this region.[31] Most of Russia's petroleum reserves are offshore. Drilling underwater requires more advanced technology than extraction on land, and the recent economic sanctions have already slowed Russian producers' access to the technology and capital needed for Arctic development. In 2014, the International Energy Agency estimated Russia would need to invest $100 billion a year for twenty years to modernize its energy sector.[32]

During the Soviet period, government policy encouraged people to move north and work in the oil and mining industries, thus Russia accounts for a large percentage of the Arctic population, many of whom live in industrial centers. Like many other parts of the country, Russia's Arctic region has suffered a drop in population since the end of the Cold War, but is still relatively populated compared to parts of the North American Arctic.[33]Although the industrial economy of the Russian Arctic is not as robust as it was previously, Russian strategy for the long term includes eventual development of resources, as well as the construction of necessary port and security infrastructure to allow shipping of commodities to markets east and west.[34] Escorting this traffic is a major rationale for Russia to increase the number of its icebreakers. Russia may also be reinforcing its capabilities in the Arctic in expectation of greater activity in the region by non-Arctic powers, especially China.

Some experts support direct U.S.-Russian military-to-military contact, though the gravity of geopolitical strains may currently preclude such contact. Another option would be to discuss subregional, multilateral issues (rather than bilateral U.S.-Russia issues) in the NATO-Russia Council. However, the Task Force finds that, for now, the newly formed Arctic Coast Guard Forum provides a practical, operationally focused context for confidence-building with Russia on Arctic issues.

The Arctic Coast Guard Forum should also address cooperative maritime law enforcement issues. However, decision-makers should be aware that misunderstandings are more likely to arise from air and maritime military maneuvers beyond the current scope of this forum.

A mechanism within the Organization for Security and Cooperation in Europe (OSCE) could provide a model for introducing more confidence-building security measures into the Arctic Council. Borrowing from the OSCE's predecessor, the Conference on Security and Cooperation in Europe, the Arctic Council could concentrate on "baskets" of issues, enabling it to address several topics of varying degrees of political sensitivity. One of these "baskets" could be security issues in which participants can exchange announcements of exercises.

The Task Force believes that the United States should begin military-to-military talks with Russia on Arctic issues and recommends that the U.S. government develop benchmarks for what military contacts on Arctic issues would be appropriate and under what conditions. Russia's actions in Ukraine and elsewhere have strained the international fabric, and the United States, the European Union, and others maintain economic sanctions on certain Russian entities. The Task Force recommends that the United States, while preserving the tradition of nonpolitical cooperation in the Arctic, continue to monitor Russian military expansion in the region and evaluate Russia's intentions in that regard. Military-to-military talks would not be a concession, but instead would offer a practical channel to accomplish needed tasks while providing a window for U.S. interlocutors to gain a better understanding of Russian intentions in the Arctic.

CHINA

In recent years, China has begun staking a claim in the Arctic. China has invested in mines in Greenland and is now negotiating a free trade deal with Iceland.[35] China is also enhancing its maritime presence and capabilities by building ice-breaking research vessels, extending its fishing fleets, and increasing maritime transportation. For instance, in September 2015, Chinese naval ships sailed around the Bering Sea. Although such a voyage is considered an innocent passage under UNCLOS, it was of interest to U.S. observers because of concerns about China's expanding naval activity in the Pacific. Additionally, China has encouraged its commercial shippers to try Arctic routes. The Chinese military has also made progress in building its own fleet of icebreakers, including the *Xue Long* and the newly unveiled *Haibing* 722, and is now building a third.[36]

The Task Force finds that there is scope for greater inclusion of China, an increasingly important player in the Arctic, in regional cooperative mechanisms. The National Science Foundation (NSF) and the Chinese Arctic and Antarctic Administration are exploring areas of further scientific collaboration.[37] China was among the twenty-five countries that participated in the September 2016 White House Arctic Science Ministerial and signed the joint statement on scientific cooperation. The Task Force finds that though China is not yet a significant power in the Arctic, its ambitions in the region merit careful attention.

CANADA

As a neighbor and close ally, Canada is well placed to work with the United States on Arctic affairs. The Task Force finds that cooperation with Canada provides an opportunity to enhance U.S. policy in the Arctic. The two countries are integral to each other's security and collaborate often, for example, through the deeply integrated North American Aerospace Defense Command (NORAD) and search and rescue efforts. Although U.S.-Canada relations remain close, the two countries disagree on the status of the waters of the Arctic Archipelago. What the United States labels as the international seas of the Northwest Passage, Canada considers to be within its sovereignty. Nevertheless, these friendly neighboring countries have been able to manage this long-standing, bilateral disagreement in peaceful and practical ways. Although U.S. policymakers have legitimate concerns about setting a precedent for coastal countries to close international straits to maritime traffic, the Task Force believes that the United States and Canada should seek to resolve their border dispute in the Beaufort Sea. Resolution of this border issue through peaceful negotiation would have a worldwide demonstration effect and also reinforce both countries' shared interests in cooperation in the North American Arctic.

U.S. MILITARY

Within the broader context of national security, U.S. national military defense includes the protection of Alaska and passage of naval vessels in—and often under—the ice-covered Arctic Ocean and important straits such as the Bering Strait. U.S. military forces also protect U.S. economic activities and facilities in the Far North, including the Alaska pipeline and large mining sites such as the Red Dog Mine. The United States has operated submarines under the Arctic since the passage of the USS *Nautilus* in 1958. Both the U.S. Navy and Coast Guard operate in the region, the latter leading federal law enforcement in the region and focused on safety, security, coastal resupply, and fisheries enforcement in the Bering Sea and the U.S. EEZ in the Arctic Ocean. The Navy completed a force structure assessment in December 2016.[38] The United States needs to determine which military forces to array in the region and how to interpret the actions of others in the region, including North Korea, whose long-range missiles may be able to strike Alaska.

The intersection of Arctic and transatlantic issues highlights how the remits of the Pacific, Northern, and European Commands converge in the Arctic region. The U.S. Department of Defense should ensure that the seams between Pacific Command (PACOM), Northern Command, and European Command are not gaps. Under the Unified Command Plan (UCP), NORTHCOM is designated the advocate for the Arctic, but shares the responsibility of defense with EUCOM. However, the majority of forces in Alaska come under the operational control of PACOM. When NORTHCOM activates Joint Task Force–Alaska, it sources its manpower from those PACOM units. This possible conflict in control has the potential for tension between combatant commanders and should be resolved in the UCP. Other than Russia's, foreign military presence in the Arctic is quite small. For the foreseeable future, most of the threats in the Arctic are derived from resource extraction activities (mining and oil and gas), illegal fishing, search and rescue challenges, and the presence of foreign commercial shipping, which may not be suitable for the harsh Arctic environment. Because this is mostly a homeland defense type of mission, NORTHCOM should be tasked with overall area responsibilities given its current domestic and homeland defense focus.

ICEBREAKERS

Perhaps the most widely debated capacity issue is the U.S. need for polar ice-breaking ships. Although Russia and other countries have numerous ice-breaking vessels, U.S. policy should not be driven by competition but by U.S. needs—and the needs are real. Greater military, commercial, scientific, and tourist activity in the region demands greater search and rescue, monitoring, and surveillance capabilities. U.S. polar icebreakers, operated by the coast guard, provide U.S. maritime and sovereign presence in Arctic and Antarctic waters as well as enforcement capacity. Each year, the United States uses an icebreaker to help resupply McMurdo Station in Antarctica. For Russia, icebreakers are not only an operational necessity, but also an income-generating service to commercial vessels plying their Arctic waters.

Ice-breaking capability will be required for a range of maritime missions. The federal government needs icebreakers for sovereign presence, law enforcement, response, science support, and other duties.[39] The coast guard may have additional work for an icebreaker related to enforcing the IMO's Polar Code, the International Code for Ships Operating in Polar Waters, which entered into effect on January 1, 2017. During the Cold War, the United States maintained up to eight true polar vessels, but today the United States has only one operational heavy icebreaker.[40] Commissioned in 1976, the *Polar Star* has exceeded its planned thirty-year service life. The aging icebreaker was refurbished and reactivated in 2012 to operate for another seven to ten years, stretching its use to 2022. The companion *Polar Sea* was commissioned in 1978, but an engine fault sidelined the ship in 2010. The United States also operates a medium-weight icebreaker, the *Healy*. Whereas heavy icebreakers, as defined by the coast guard, can break through ice six-feet thick at a continuous speed of three knots, the *Healy* can break through ice four-and-a-half-feet thick at three knots.[41] The NSF also leases two polar research ships for Antarctic operations, the *Nathaniel Palmer* and the *Laurence Gould*. These national roles for icebreakers differ from commercial operations and escorting of commercial ships.

With simultaneous, long-term commitments in the Arctic and the Antarctic, the United States should commit to building more than one icebreaker in the next decade as part of enhancing its global capabilities. Difficult design decisions will need to be made to build the new icebreakers. The U.S. Coast Guard Acquisition Directorate currently advises that the coast guard requires a minimum of three operational heavy icebreakers to support U.S. security, economic, and commercial needs.[42] However, the 2010 high latitude region mission analysis report, affirmed by a Department of Homeland Security mission needs statement in 2013, concludes that the coast guard requires three heavy as well as three medium icebreakers to fulfill its statutory missions.[43] The Task Force recommends that the U.S. Congress approve funding for building up to six icebreakers so that sufficient capacity is available for active duty at both poles given maintenance schedules. After this initial investment, additional icebreakers can be built more easily. The Obama administration requested $150 million in FY 2017 funding for the latest tranche of icebreaker modernization. In the legislative process, the defense subcommittee of the U.S. Senate Committee on Appropriations added $1 billion to build one new icebreaker. Even with significant funding, building an icebreaker takes up to ten years. If a new icebreaker were first funded in FY 2017 and construction began in FY 2020, the ship could potentially be completed in 2024 or 2025.[44]

In the interim, U.S. policymakers could consider alternatives if there were to be a gap in coast guard polar icebreaker operations. Experts argue that the Jones Act, which regulates maritime commerce between U.S. cities, precludes leasing vessels from another country.[45] The Task Force finds that icebreakers are a national capacity, which the United States should build on its own, but suggests that policymakers consider leasing additional icebreakers from the U.S. private sector until new ships can be built. Just as the National Aeronautics and Space Administration (NASA) accesses outer space via rockets owned by private companies, the coast guard could use U.S.-flagged private sector ships as an interim measure until new national capacity is available.

In addition to building and maintaining its own icebreakers, the United States could also support a cooperative international ice-breaking unit. The Arctic coastal countries could create a unit with assets or personnel from several countries to help with ice breaking in the Arctic high seas. Some countries could contribute ships, and others, such as the United States, could contribute logistical or communications assistance. Currently, the United States conducts joint ice-breaking activities on the Great Lakes with Canada, which could serve as a model for greater international cooperation, although this effort is easier because they are close allies.

SEARCH AND RESCUE

Safe navigation in the Arctic is important to the United States. The United States, like all littoral countries, has an obligation to rescue those in trouble in its seas. Governments, acting together at the International Maritime Organization, have adopted a new Polar Code, which offers detailed requirements for enhanced safety standards for ship structure, navigation, fire safety, and other procedures for operations in the extreme cold in the Arctic and the Antarctic.[46] All five Arctic coastal states are members of the IMO Council, which adopted the measure and have a special interest in mariners' adherence to these standards. Under IMO rules, the country of registration should certify that vessels meet legal standards. However, flags of convenience, in which a ship flies the flag of a country other than the country of ownership, may not be prepared to conduct the extensive examinations to confirm strict adherence to the Polar Code. Under the principle of port state control, a country can enforce standards if a ship is entering its port, thus the United States can enforce maritime rules on those that declare intent to enter a U.S. port but cannot stop transit traffic.

The Task Force supports the Polar Code but believes that Arctic states need to work together to implement and enforce these new international maritime standards. For instance, because ships passing through the Bering Strait may stop at ports in Russia, the United States, or Canada, the U.S. government could work with its Russian and Canadian counterparts, along with insurance companies, to enforce the Polar Code by inspecting ships entering their ports. These cooperative efforts may help build a climate of compliance with the code, and the program could later be expanded to all coastal Arctic states.

CUSTOMS AND IMMIGRATION

Half of the U.S. coastline is Alaskan. With 6,640 miles of coastline—33,904 miles including islands—Alaska has a longer coastline than all of the other forty-nine states put together.[47] The Alaska coastline is both a national and state border, and the city of Nome is the first port of entry to the United States along the northwest coast. However, as of 2016, the Customs and Border Protection presence was quite small, which presents a potential problem because the shallow waters off the Alaska coast could make it possible for individuals to leave a ship and enter the United States illegally. The Task Force recommends that the Department of Homeland Security allocate additional personnel to be stationed in Nome.

ARCTIC COUNCIL

Presently, the Arctic Council excludes military security issues from its remit, enabling it to focus on environmental protection and sustainable development issues. As human activity increases in the region, the member states will need to work harder to preserve the cooperative spirit of the body and determine whether the current governance architecture of the council is sufficient. Some observers assert that the Arctic Council's scope should be expanded to include military and security issues. Its history of cooperative relations could provide a positive environment for discussing more sensitive military security issues. Conversely, this cooperative practice could be undermined by adding adversarial strategic issues to the Arctic Council's agenda. The eight countries are all members of other bodies, including the OSCE and the United Nations. However, these entities are large and cover a wide range of issues that would distract from the focus on the Arctic.

The Task Force finds that the Arctic Council addresses scientific and environmental issues well and facilitates effective cooperation among indigenous peoples. The Task Force recommends that the Arctic Council consider greater non-warfighting security measures, such as search and rescue and oil spill recovery. Arctic Council members will also need to consider the financial structure of the organization, which operates on voluntary funding from its member states.

FINDINGS AND RECOMMENDATIONS FOR ENHANCING U.S. NATIONAL SECURITY IN THE ARCTIC

The Task Force finds that

- the United States has important security and national defense interests in the Arctic;

- the United States should maintain its Arctic underwater naval capacities;
- interpretation of Russian intentions will influence U.S. policy in the region;
- cooperation with Canada is an important component of U.S. capacity in the Arctic;
- icebreakers are a national capacity;
- the United States needs to invest in improved domain awareness for national security and economic activity;
- managing safe transit through the Bering Strait and near the coast is in the national interest;
- increased tourist and commercial traffic necessitates an increased presence of the Department of Homeland Security in the region;
- Alaska provides a staging point for U.S. military operations in the Pacific; and
- the U.S. chairmanship of the Arctic Council from 2015 to 2017 has been a useful vehicle for increasing national policymakers' attention to the region and has reinforced the Arctic Council as the premier international organization in the region.

The Task Force recommends that the United States

- fund and maintain up to six icebreakers in the coming decade to meet simultaneous commitments in the Arctic and Antarctic;
- build its icebreakers in U.S. shipyards;
- consider creating a cooperative international ice-breaking unit with other Arctic countries;
- explore the modalities of military-to-military talks with Russia in conjunction with the Arctic Security Forces Roundtable;
- resolve overlaps and gaps among EUCOM, NORTHCOM, and PACOM in the UCP and task NORTHCOM with overall area responsibilities;
- complement NORAD's air defense system with an updated land and sea alert system;
- give higher priority to resolving the U.S.-Canada border dispute in the Beaufort Sea;

- support more confidence-building security measures in the Arctic Council, probably in the Arctic Coast Guard Forum;
- work with other Arctic countries and insurance companies to enforce the mandatory Polar Code on all ships entering nearby national ports;
- consider creating an internationally staffed joint search and rescue operations center with other Arctic countries;
- station additional customs and immigration personnel in Nome, Alaska; and
- implement the U.S. Coast Guard's proposed initiative to publish voluntary routes through the Bering Strait on a chart.

Economic, Energy, and Environmental Interests

Economic, energy, and environmental issues are entwined in the Arctic. Energy and natural resource extraction are the primary economic activities, and tourism is a growing sector. U.S. economic interests in the Arctic include both activities in the region and passage through it, with economic possibilities including maritime transportation, energy, mining, fisheries, and the development of Alaskan communities. Given the region's burgeoning potential, the Arctic Economic Council was created in 2014 as a venue for international business-to-business cooperation to promote prosperity and sustainable development.

Building on U.S. strengths in technology would help the United States bolster its economic potential across these activities. It would also bring benefits on the state and local level because the state of Alaska needs economic diversification and Alaska Native subsistence hunters need protected spaces. Although most of the region's economic development will come from private efforts, the Task Force recommends that the U.S. government focus public funds on infrastructure development and additional scientific evaluation that would benefit many residents and several industries, and on improving the integrity and well-being of disadvantaged communities, which do not have ample resources to grapple with changing conditions.

OIL AND GAS

The Arctic is rich in natural resources, and oil and gas in the region are part of the strategic assets available to the United States. Although these resources are potentially substantial, they would need to be proven via further exploration activities.

Containing an estimated 13 percent, or 90 billion barrels, of the world's undiscovered conventional oil resources and 30 percent of its undiscovered conventional natural gas resources, the Arctic offers significant energy opportunities.[48] Half of these energy resources are located in Alaska, and of those, the U.S. Geological Survey estimates thirty billion barrels of oil and 181 trillion cubic feet of gas may be technically recoverable.[49]

Yet the economic drivers of the oil and gas industry have shifted. A 2015 National Petroleum Council report to the Department of Energy, which had requested a comprehensive study on the research and technology opportunities that would enable prudent development of U.S. Arctic oil and gas resources, detailed these changes.[50] Production from other large oil sources, such as shale oil, and the discovery of large Brazilian offshore pre-salt deposits, have reduced the demand for more challenging hydrocarbon resources such as those in the Arctic. The current low-price stage of the commodity cycle further reduces the economic incentives to pursue these resources now.

Thus, the more distant, Arctic offshore resources are not needed now and do not need to be pursued immediately. But the United States should recognize it possesses these strategic resources in the event that supply and demand or geopolitical events create the conditions for them to be developed. In this context, it is important to consider two factors. First, production from these resources is a long-term proposition, and considering the physical development and regulatory requirements, meaningful supply into the market could take fifteen to twenty years, following a sustained exploration program. This prospect gives the United States time to further develop its technologies for oil and gas extraction and environmental protection. Second, nearly all of the recommendations in this report—including on environmental science, infrastructure, and response capabilities, among others—would support these efforts if development of these resources were to occur in the future.

For decades, Alaska has been a major source of oil and gas, and the Trans Alaska Pipeline System (TAPS) has carried petroleum from the North Slope to the Valdez Marine Terminal since 1977 (map 2). Depletion of previously discovered resources (mainly Prudhoe Bay) has resulted in reduced flowrates via TAPS. TAPS is one of the world's largest pipeline systems, and at its peak, the pipeline contributed significant revenue to the state. Pipeline throughput peaked in 1988 at more than two million barrels a day, and TAPS was delivering 25 percent of all U.S. oil production. By 2016, the pipeline was moving less than five hundred thousand barrels a day, only a quarter of its highest rate.[51] Earlier in the year, TAPS provided about 8 percent of U.S. oil production, which dropped to 6.4 percent in September 2016.[52] Further reducing throughput will increase operational challenges as it becomes harder to keep the pipeline warm and functioning properly in very cold weather. If the TAPS throughput were discontinued, it would likely be difficult to restart, and the United States could lose a critical piece of energy supply infrastructure. The Trump administration should reflect on this possibility and ensure the appropriate studies for options to maintain TAPS are being executed.

In 2015, after drilling the first well in Alaska's outer continental shelf since the early 1990s, Royal Dutch Shell, the company most active in exploring offshore drilling, discontinued operations, citing high costs, shifting global opportunities, and regulatory uncertainty. Several other major oil and gas firms have abandoned most of their leases in the Arctic. The Obama administration subsequently canceled the auction of Arctic offshore drilling leases for the next two years.[53] The Department of the Interior's 2017 to 2022 lease sale schedule includes ten sites, with one in Alaska's Cook Inlet but none offshore in the Arctic Ocean.[54]

The United States will need to assess how and to what extent it might use Arctic assets to meet energy needs while protecting vulnerable areas. In November 2016, an Alaska Native corporation, the Arctic Slope Regional Corporation, purchased the lease areas that Shell had vacated.[55] In December 2016, the Obama administration banned drilling for oil in the majority of the Chukchi and Beaufort Seas.[56] However, the ban remains in effect only in federally controlled Arctic waters and does not affect drilling in state-controlled waters.

Risks of catastrophic environmental damage from oil spills are numerous. Although U.S. companies operating offshore drilling rigs follow high standards for the industry, accidents can still happen. The TAPS also claims a long history of careful management, but risks remain. The AESC has tasked the Department of Homeland Security and U.S. Coast Guard with developing more extensive plans to prevent and respond to oil spills in the Arctic region.

Moreover, adherence to high industry standards is not uniform across the Arctic, despite recent efforts. In 2013, via the Arctic Council, the ministers of the Arctic states signed the Agreement on Cooperation

MAP 2: MAP OF ALASKA

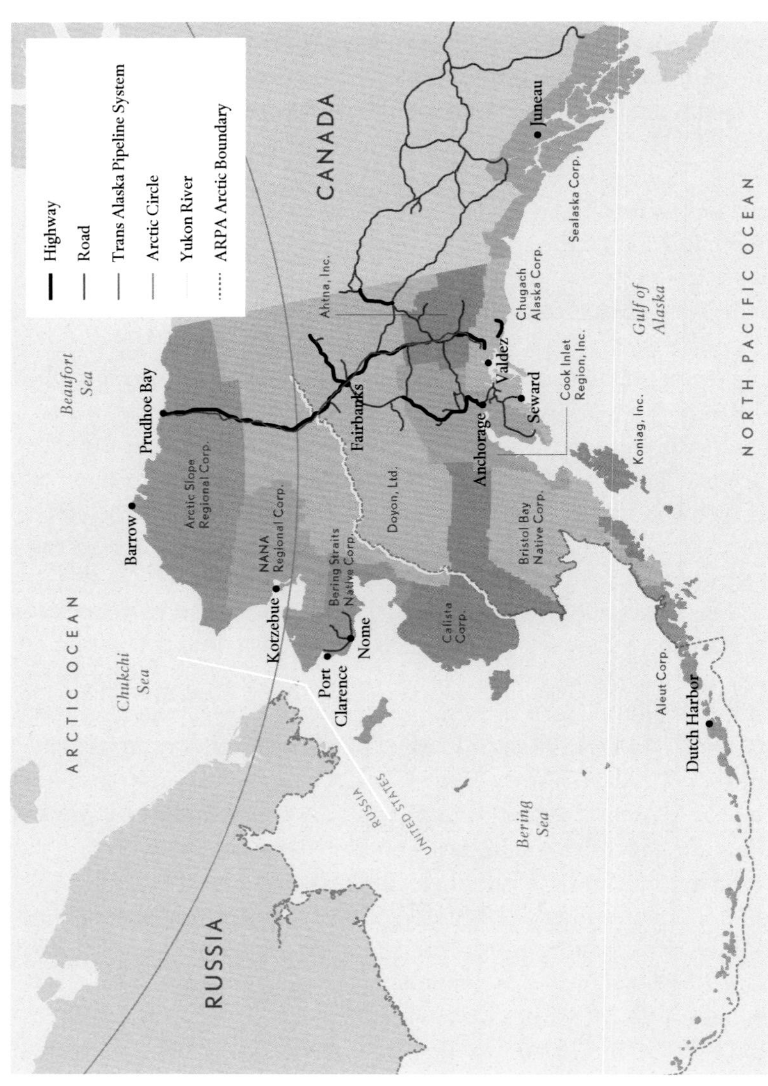

on Marine Oil Pollution Preparedness and Response in the Arctic, a legally binding measure. Similarly, the 2016 U.S.-Canada joint statement included commitments to enhance cooperation on clean energy. The recently created Arctic Offshore Regulators Forum, a suborganization of the Arctic Council, met in 2015 and again in 2016 to discuss safety in the oil industry. The Task Force finds that these are useful frameworks, but strong safety enforcement by national governments will be needed for such agreements to be effective. The United States should be a leader in setting the standard for development in the Arctic, giving full consideration for protecting the environment and the people who rely on it.

In addition to furthering efforts in science and technology related to protecting the Arctic environment from risks such as oil spills, alternative sources of energy for regions in the Arctic, including Alaska, remain critical to resolving energy challenges. Many Alaskan communities currently use expensive and environmentally taxing sources of fuel to provide the power they need. For instance, an extensive riverine fuel delivery system involves lightering or hoses to bring diesel fuel to Alaska Native communities in the Northwest Borough and the North Slope. The delicacy of the environment and the difficulty of energy delivery in the harsh conditions make the Arctic region a prime candidate for renewable energy.

In recent years, U.S. Arctic strategy has included clean energy measures, such as increased solar and wind generation, to displace some diesel demand in remote communities. The Task Force supports these measures but is concerned that implementation and funding will lessen over time. Although it would take years to recoup the investment costs, this burden is an inherent part of shifting to a more sustainable economic platform. Further, Alaska has become a leader in developing innovative, off-grid renewable energy technologies—the Alaska Center for Energy and Power and the Alaska Renewable Energy Project being prime examples—and could become an exporter of knowledge and know-how. The Task Force finds that the Arctic could serve as an incubator for energy innovation. Greater use of renewables would reduce dependence on costly diesel fuel, which produces harmful emissions and has detrimental effects on health. New technological developments in nuclear energy, such as small modular reactors, also offer an opportunity for economic development in the region while reducing dependence on fossil fuels.

ENVIRONMENTAL CONCERNS

The Arctic is a remarkable region, encompassing vast areas of intact marine and terrestrial habitats, some of the roughest seas in the world, an extreme and variable climate, diverse human cultures whose traditions are closely tied to the bounty of the land and sea, and abundant wildlife. The rich Arctic environment attracts significant wildlife to the region, including millions of birds from every continent each year, bowhead whales from the Bering Sea, and gray whales from Mexico.

As the Arctic sea ice declines, resources that were once remote and difficult to access are becoming increasingly accessible, opening not only the way to new commerce but also new risks. For instance, ship hulls and holds, in addition to sewage and other discharge from these vessels, can carry invasive species into Arctic waters. In 2004, member states adopted the IMO's International Convention for the Control and Management of Ships' Ballast Water and Sediments. Having received sufficient ratifications, the measure enters into force on September 8, 2017. Additionally, noise from passing ships can disorient marine mammals and make them change their routes. Changing migration patterns, in turn, affect the animals and the Alaska Natives who harvest them. As economic activity in the region increases, the Task Force finds that the United States will need sustained policies supported by scientific data and evaluation to support culturally and environmentally sensitive economic development.

The sea is a major focus of environmental conservation efforts, but the air in the Arctic matters as well. Thawing permafrost releases carbon and methane, both greenhouse gases. A pound of methane can trap twenty-five to thirty-three times more heat than a pound of carbon dioxide.[57] Norway has already developed technology for methane capture, and the United States should follow its example and invest in state-of-the-art methane capture technology as well. In 2015, the Arctic Council created an experts group to monitor implementation of the council's framework for action on black carbon and methane by its members. The Task Force recommends that Arctic Council members urge observer states to adopt the framework.[58]

At some oil and gas production sites across the world, natural gas is burned off or "flared," releasing more than three hundred million tons of carbon dioxide annually, as well as black carbon, into the atmosphere.[59] The Task Force supports the World Bank's Zero Routine

Flaring by 2030 initiative, which brings together governments, oil companies, and NGOs and calls for natural gas to be conserved or used but not wasted by flaring.

The Task Force recommends that the United States and other Arctic countries convene a high-level international panel of leading scientists and policymakers tasked with helping world leaders avert Arctic and other warming-related tipping points. This panel would lead an urgent initiative to identify the timing, triggers, and consequences of Arctic and global thresholds that the climate cannot cross without having serious implications for people across the planet. The panel would also identify monitoring gaps that should be filled to better understand Arctic warming thresholds. Last, it would strive to recommend to world leaders the amount of Arctic permafrost, sea ice, glaciers, ice sheets, and other conditions that should be preserved to avoid unstoppable and dire effects.

Even beyond the Arctic countries, global leaders are addressing how to operate in the Arctic. In December 2015, the World Economic Forum issued its "Arctic Investment Protocol: Guidelines for Responsible Investing in the Arctic," which stresses sustainability and the inclusion of indigenous peoples.[60]

MARITIME TRANSPORTATION

The reduction in ice opens the ocean to navigation (map 3). The possibility of new sea lanes is important for global trade; 90 percent of world trade moves by sea.[61] The quest for shorter sea transportation routes has propelled strategy and politics for centuries. Sailing from China to Europe through the Arctic Ocean could reduce the distance significantly over sailing through the Indian Ocean. Analysts estimate that an Arctic route from Shanghai to Hamburg would save 2,800 nautical miles over a Suez Canal route if the waters are ice free and operating conditions were much like the open ocean.[62]

However, the economic viability of trans-Arctic maritime transportation is unclear. In a world of just-in-time manufacturing, shippers need to guarantee delivery on schedule, and mileage and ship speeds affect comparative delivery times. Capricious Arctic weather also makes planning travel time difficult. A delay of just one day could be too expensive for customers to bear. The economics of an Arctic route

MAP 3: ARCTIC SEA ICE EXTENT AND SEA ROUTES

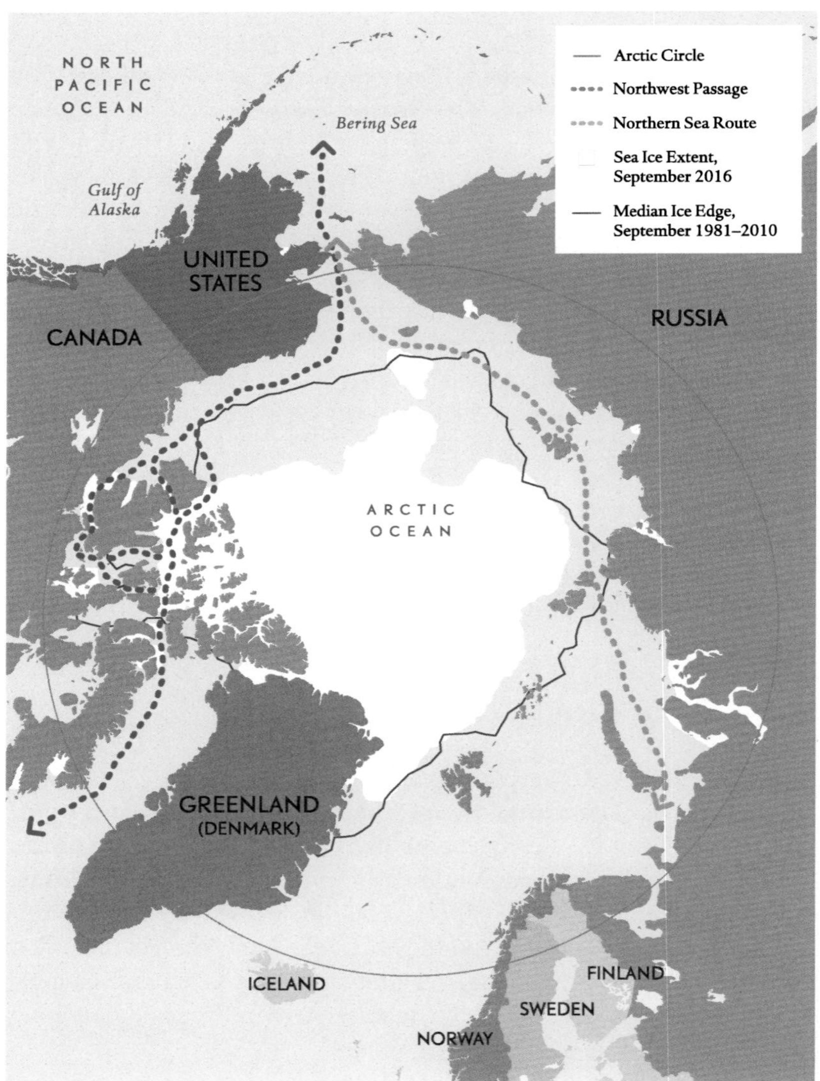

Source: F. Fetterer, K. Knowles, W. Meier, and M. Savoie, Sea Ice Index, Version 2 (Boulder, CO: National Snow and Ice Data Center, 2016), https://nsidc.org/data/g02135#.

should be compared with the alternatives. Improvements in other routes, such as the expansion of the Panama Canal in June 2016 and Suez Canal in 2015, affect the calculus. The value of the commodities being transported and the fuel to move them also affects the economics of commercial shipping.

The Task Force finds that optimism about new Arctic sea lanes needs to be tempered by the difficult realities of operating in the Arctic. A melting sea ice cover does not mean an ice-free open ocean. Ships could encounter poor conditions in regions that previously were ice covered. Mariners and insurance companies—as well as the coast guards who conduct search and rescue—want shippers to adhere to the high standards required to operate in such a harsh environment. The IMO has developed a Polar Code to promote safe operations in the Arctic and Antarctic. Recognizing the need for greater cooperation for search and rescue, the Arctic Council countries adopted their first legally binding agreement in 2011 with the conclusion of the Agreement on Cooperation on Aeronautical and Maritime Search and Rescue in the Arctic and the Agreement on Cooperation on Marine Oil Pollution Preparedness and Response in 2013. The Task Force supports these measures and urges Arctic states to implement and enforce them.

In addition to mariners, visitors are also venturing farther into the region. Cruise ship companies offer to sail adventurous tourists through the more open—yet still icy—waters. The *Crystal Serenity*, the largest cruise ship to traverse the Northwest Passage, successfully sailed from Anchorage to New York in summer 2016, and additional Arctic cruises are already planned for 2017 and beyond.

Yet even a modest increase in maritime activity places pressure on infrastructure in the American Arctic. The Northern Sea route, the Northwest Passage, and even a potential transpolar route would all pass through the Bering Strait, which at its narrowest is fifty-five miles wide and at its shallowest is ninety-eight feet deep.[63] Two islands in the Bering Strait, Big Diomede in Russia and Little Diomede in the United States, narrow the distance between the two countries to just two and a half miles.[64] This region is one of the most environmentally sensitive marine areas in the world. Any incident in this region—an accident, fuel spill, or even maritime waste discharge—would affect the coasts of both countries. Increased transit traffic only increases the risk of mishap. Also, search and rescue capabilities are limited in the region, and it would take days or even weeks to reach a vessel in distress. To address these limitations, the Task Force urges more safe harbor and search and rescue stations be situated along the Alaska coast.

On December 9, 2016, President Obama signed an executive order creating a Northern Bering Sea Climate Resilience Area of 112,300 square miles. The executive order also provided a framework for working with Alaska Natives to protect the area's environment and wildlife from the threats of increased maritime traffic in this region. Among its components, the framework calls for the U.S. Coast Guard to publish a Bering port access route study, requires the Bering task force to recommend ways to implement the IMO's Polar Code, creates a Bering intergovernmental tribal advisory council, and withdraws designated areas on the outer continental shelf from leasing.[65] The Task Force supports further implementation of the resilience area measures as a way to secure U.S. interests as international traffic increases in this narrow passageway.

INFRASTRUCTURE

One of the foundations of U.S. power, prosperity, and identity is know-how. From the Industrial Revolution to the invention of the internet, science and technology have been important components of U.S. leadership, and this blend of strategy, science, and exploration has been a critical feature of U.S. activity in the Arctic for more than a century. In 1957, three U.S. Coast Guard cutters completed the first circumnavigation of North America voyaging through the fabled Northwest Passage, and today the United States remains a leader in polar science. In spite of these achievements, the United States lags in other aspects.

Almost no marine infrastructure is in place within the U.S. maritime Arctic. In some areas, infrastructure was provided by the oil and gas industry to support their facilities, and their departure has thrust public needs back on public authorities at the local, state, and national level. Potential commercial activity would be hampered by inadequate infrastructure. Deepwater ports exist in Norway, Iceland, and Russia, the largest of which is in Murmansk, Russia, but the North American Arctic has no major port to service transoceanic maritime transportation. The port at Nome, Alaska, is only twenty-two feet deep, but the city of Nome hopes to build out its docks to reach a draft of thirty-five feet deep without dredging.[66] The Army Corps of Engineers defines a deepwater port as forty-five feet deep.[67] A possible alternative could be to locate a new harbor at Port Clarence, which served as a U.S. Coast Guard LORAN C radio navigation station until 2010, when the system was terminated in favor of the newer Global Positioning System (GPS).[68] The Task Force urges policymakers to reinforce U.S. strategic presence in the Arctic by making a sustained commitment to boosting technology and building the infrastructure for safe operations in the region.

The U.S. Congress has begun to consider legislation on a port, with the introduction of House Resolution 5978, the Coast Guard and Maritime Transportation Amendments Act of 2016, and the Senate's approval of the Water Resources Development Act, which includes $1.4 billion over five years for infrastructure and a deep draft Arctic port, as well as subsistence harbors, including one on Little Diomede.[69] It is not clear that a new deepwater port would cause a significant increase in transoceanic shipping or that vessels would be pulling into Alaskan ports. Arctic shipping may be mostly destination-driven, moving natural resources out of the Arctic using bulk carriers and tankers, with many vessels bypassing Alaska entirely. As the Arctic Council's Arctic marine shipping assessment noted, half of shipping in the region follows the North Pacific great circle route through the Aleutian Islands.[70] The future of Arctic shipping is more closely linked to the development of Arctic natural resources and their movement out of the Arctic to global markets.[71] The Task Force urges completion of an up-to-date analysis of locations, first, for safe harbor ports for subsistence hunters and coast guard search and rescue and, second, for a deepwater port in Alaska.

If a deepwater port in Alaska were dredged, it would need to be sustained by connections on land. Presently, however, northern and northwestern Alaska have few paved roads and no railroads. An important reason for having a U.S. Arctic port is for the export of Alaska's natural resources, and intermodal transportation systems would be critical to moving these resources to ports and then to global markets. Even if commercial transshipment does not increase dramatically, tourism will. Passengers on the *Crystal Serenity*, for example, disembarked at several northern locations using ferries. The luxury cruise ship was accompanied by its own search and rescue and ice-breaking ship, and its captain was in contact with coastal authorities. As tourism intensifies, future cruises may not take the time or spend the money to be so well prepared. Even a modest increase in maritime traffic puts great pressure on search and rescue capabilities. The Task Force's recommendation of creating a series of safe harbor and search and rescue stations along the coast would be integral to improving infrastructure in the region and preparing for potential traffic increases, whether from transshipment, tourism, or both.

MAPPING AND WEATHER

Further complicating the rise in maritime activity in the region is the reality that parts of the Arctic Ocean are not well charted. According to NOAA's hydrographic services review panel, an advisory group on the U.S. marine transportation system, only 4.7 percent of the U.S. maritime Arctic is currently charted to modern international standards.[72] On land, the U.S. Geological Survey works with the government of Alaska on the Alaska Mapping Initiative, using high resolution data to update maps. In 2015, the Obama administration announced collaboration among the National Geospatial-Intelligence Agency, the NSF, and the University of Minnesota's Polar Geospatial Center to create digital elevation models of Alaska in 2016 and later of the Arctic as a whole.[73] The result is unprecedented: high resolution, frequently refreshed satellite imagery of the Arctic available to the public.

Arctic weather prediction is also difficult despite recent international efforts to enhance weather prediction capabilities. In 2011, the World Meteorological Congress launched the Global Integrated Polar Prediction System (GIPPS) under the auspices of the World Meteorological Organization (WMO), which is supported by the WMO's Polar Prediction Project and the World Climate Research Program's Polar Climate Predictability Initiative. The Polar Prediction Project has designated mid-2017 to mid-2019 as the Year of Polar Prediction, seeking to improve environmental prediction capabilities through a coordinated period of intensive observing, modeling, verification, user engagement, and education activities. The Task Force believes that the United States should invest in additional weather measurement capacity and continue to support international cooperation in weather prediction.

Economic, energy, and environmental changes are interconnected in the Arctic. For years, oil companies drilling offshore have worked with Alaska Native communities to avoid sailing tankers where people are conducting subsistence hunting and fishing. The Task Force finds that policymakers, mariners, and the public would benefit from integrated information. The University of Alaska or a similar research organization could consolidate information collected by several other groups to create charts of animal migration and maritime traffic. Organizations such as the Audubon Society have been mapping the migration of birds and whales around Alaska, the U.S. Coast Guard tracks maritime transportation, and Alaska Natives track marine mammals and fish. The Task Force suggests that the creation of maps in which different types of information were overlaid could help clarify no-go areas, which would help protect Alaska Natives' economic well-being and support safe commercial navigation.

TELECOMMUNICATIONS

Improving telecommunications technology should be an important part of U.S. strategy in the Arctic. Telecommunications links are currently poor throughout parts of the Arctic. Satellites supporting the U.S. GPS orbit at an inclination of 55 degrees, favoring coverage for lower latitudes. The Russian GLONASS system provides better coverage in the Arctic; its satellites orbit at 64.8 degrees.[74] Users in the Arctic do not benefit significantly from the satellite-based augmentation system (SBAS), which is located in geostationary orbit over the equator. The SBAS's GPS correction signal is poor in the Arctic and is not receivable above 81 degrees north.[75] Better interconnections among GPS, GLONASS, the European Union's Galileo Global Navigation Satellite System, China's BeiDou Navigation Satellite System, India's regional Navigation With Indian Constellation (NAVIC), and Japan's regional Quasi-Zenith Satellite System (QZSS) would be beneficial. The Task Force finds that improved communications is crucial for navigation and search and rescue, as well as for contacts among residents and with the rest of the world.

Communications are most developed in the Nordic Arctic, next in the Russian Arctic, and least in the North American Arctic. However, private companies are beginning to build new networks in the U.S. Arctic. For example, in 2016, Quintillion, an Anchorage-based telecommunications company, began laying a repeated submarine fiber optic cable that will run through the Bering Strait and along the Alaska coast, with lines branching to Alaska cities. Iridium, a satellite communications company, provides some voice and data coverage in the Arctic region, but circumpolar communications links are still few. The Task Force believes that developing a trans-Arctic search and rescue communications network would be an important improvement that benefits both residents and visitors. For example, better internet or mobile telephone links would enable sick people in remote areas to be diagnosed via telemedicine links or allow teachers to connect with students for long-distance learning opportunities.

Other potential opportunities for improved communication are available. In the lower forty-eight states, the U.S. Coast Guard operates a very high frequency (VHF) emergency radio frequency, which is available twenty miles from shore. Presently, the system is not available in Alaska, but the coast guard and Federal Communications Commission could develop a similar system suitable for the Arctic. Additionally, the Alaska Arctic Waterway Safety Committee was created in 2014 and includes a network of Alaska Natives from the northwestern part of the state who are working on proposals for improved communications.[76]

A major obstacle to improving telecommunications infrastructure in the Arctic is the great expense and difficulty involved. Telecommunications improvements may necessitate new mechanisms on the ground or orbiting in space. Policymakers will need to set priorities and explore what costs should be borne by governments and what should be led by the private sector or through partnerships.

EXTRACTION

The harsh yet delicate Arctic environment yields copper, nickel, iron, gold, and other valuable minerals and metals. The Red Dog Mine in Alaska is one of the largest zinc and lead mines in the world, and Russia's Norilsk Nickel complex is the largest nickel and palladium mine in the world and the fourth largest copper mine. Diminishing sea ice may allow for greater marine access to mining, which could bring wealth but also disrupt natural habitats. Conversely, melting of permafrost could reduce land access to some mining areas. Rare earth metals may also be a lucrative industry in the Arctic and provide competition to China, which currently controls more than 40 percent of the world's rare earth reserves and still produces about 89 percent of the global rare earth elements output.[77] At times, China has restricted exports, significantly driving up world prices, and a new market could help to lessen the dependency on Chinese rare earth metals.[78]

However, global commodities prices, now low, will influence whether Arctic mining will be developed further. The city of Nome, for example, was founded during the Alaska gold rush, but dredging for gold has ebbed. The Inuit Circumpolar Council advocates for understanding of the status, role, and rights of Arctic indigenous peoples in relation to extractive industry activity.[79] The Task Force calls for the highest environmental and cultural standards for resource extraction to be examined and put in place before proceeding.

FISHING

The U.S. Arctic is rich in renewable resources, notably fisheries. Although the polar sea ice cap has historically precluded significant commercial fishing at the North Pole, most commercial and indigenous fishing occurs in the territorial waters of Arctic coastal countries. For instance, the Bering Sea provides more than half of the wild-caught fish and shellfish in the United States each year.[80] However, some commercial fishing in the high seas portion of the Arctic Ocean has been conducted by fleets from countries outside the region. Accordingly, the Arctic countries share an interest in limiting such fishing and reducing this type of traffic in the region.

Taking a precautionary approach, the coastal countries agreed not to support fishing in this region for now, although the ability to commercially fish in the Arctic is still years away. In 2009, the United States placed a moratorium on commercial fishing in its EEZ north of the Bering Strait.[81] In July 2015, all five Arctic Ocean coastal states agreed to the nonbinding Declaration Concerning the Prevention of Unregulated High Seas Fishing in the Central Arctic Ocean, stipulating that these countries would not authorize their own ships to fish in the Arctic high seas until more scientific information about the movement of fish as the ocean warms becomes available. Coastal Arctic countries want other countries with significant fishing fleets to adopt the same approach. The United States invited China, Japan, Iceland, South Korea, and the European Union to a meeting in December 2015 to discuss a permanent ban, which is supported by the government of Alaska, Alaska Natives, the Alaska fishing industry, and environmental groups.[82] Subsequent meetings were hosted in 2016 by Norway, again by the United States, and by Canada.

In their joint statement from the U.S.-Canada summit meeting in 2016, President Obama and Prime Minister Trudeau called for "a binding international agreement to prevent the opening of unregulated fisheries in the Central Arctic Ocean."[83] The Task Force commends this step and supports a permanent moratorium, which would help Alaska Native subsistence fishers and protect wildlife without significant cost to the economies of Arctic countries. Arctic indigenous peoples would need to be consulted as this policy develops. To be effective, non-Arctic actors with major fishing fleets, including China, Japan, and Taiwan, would also need to participate.

Ecosystem-based approaches offer useful examples. Marine protected areas (MPAs) are proving to be an effective management tool to conserve fisheries and other biological resources. However, other area-based management approaches are also needed in the Arctic to address goals such as food security and conservation in a dynamic system where climate effects are causing rapid changes in species distributions and ecosystem functions. Parties to the Convention on Biological Diversity, a multilateral treaty dedicated to promoting sustainable development, agreed that at least 10 percent of oceans should be managed as MPAs, and the Arctic Council nations have agreed to create a circumpolar network of MPAs. Science—both biological and social—is needed to shape new area-based management tools that will contribute to maintaining marine and coastal areas, as well as the cultures connected to them. In addition, the Arctic Council and its permanent participants could consider MPAs in its discussions. The U.S. government should seek integrated approaches to monitor the effectiveness of marine-managed areas and to allow for flexible adaptive approaches.

FINDINGS AND RECOMMENDATIONS FOR ADVANCING U.S. ECONOMIC, ENERGY, AND ENVIRONMENTAL INTERESTS IN THE ARCTIC

The Task Force finds that

- current low oil prices, as a result of the global economic slowdown and increased oil supply from non-Arctic regions, make extracting outer continental shelf Alaska resources less economically viable at this time, but their potential strategic importance should be recognized;

- increased maritime traffic, the fluctuating world energy market, and the changing environment will strain capacities in Alaska; and
- governments and companies will need to work together to improve telecommunications services in the region.

The Task Force recommends that the United States

- improve its Arctic infrastructure by
  - creating a series of safe harbor and search and rescue stations along the coast;
  - continuing to examine locations for a deepwater port;
  - developing a trans-Arctic search and rescue communications network;
  - developing a corollary in Alaska to the coast guard VHF emergency radio frequency;
  - overlaying information from different sources to create maps clarifying no-go areas; and
  - working with other Arctic countries to position more satellites in geostationary orbit over the Arctic for telecommunications and environmental monitoring;
- support the World Bank's Zero Routine Flaring by 2030 initiative and the Arctic Council's framework for action on black carbon and methane;
- extend the moratorium on commercial fishing in the central Arctic Ocean;
- consider options to maintain the long-term viability of TAPS infrastructure;
- examine and apply the highest environmental standards for resource extraction before proceeding with further mining; and
- continue supporting policies that promote environmental conservation, in addition to addressing climate change.

Alaska and Alaska Natives

The United States cannot be an effective Arctic power without addressing the security and strength of the state of Alaska. At 656,425 square miles, Alaska is the largest state, more than twice the size of Texas and one-fifth the size of the entire United States, but it also has the lowest population density in the nation. Nearly one-third of Alaska lies within the Arctic Circle. Alaska also has the longest general coastline of any state, extending for 6,640 miles, a distance greater than that of all the other states' coastlines combined. Alaska accounts for 8 percent of the oil produced in the United States, and most of America's salmon, crab, halibut, and herring come from the state.[84]

Alaska contains a unique system of multiple jurisdictions. There are boroughs that operate like counties and various Alaska Native institutions, including Alaska Native tribal governments and corporations, all of which bolster representation but can slow decision-making and diffuse responsibility.[85] Alaska Native regional and village corporations were created as part of the 1971 Alaska Native Claims Settlement Act to enable Alaska Natives to own and share the income from natural resources on their land (map 2).[86]

Despite its abundance of resources, Alaska's economy is vulnerable. The state's economy rests on three pillars: oil and gas, the federal government and the U.S. military, and everything else, including tourism and fishing. Like many petro-state countries ironically blessed with the resource curse, Alaska has benefitted from the profits of its sale of petroleum, but has not yet developed a resilient integrated economy nor a balanced tax system. Each Alaskan has shared in the bounty; a quarter of the revenue generated has been deposited in the Alaska Permanent Fund, which invests the money (valued at more than $54 billion) and pays an annual dividend to qualified Alaska residents.[87] However, the drop in global oil prices has had a devastating effect on the Alaskan economy, resulting in a large budget deficit and a lingering recession. Alaskans are now considering how to diversify their economy.

Economic, environmental, and energy needs would be addressed by improving infrastructure and by diplomatic efforts to reinforce existing cooperation among Arctic countries. Some of the infrastructure that would benefit oil and gas exploration would also benefit scientific research and commercial maritime traffic. Such measures include improved communications systems, search and rescue, oil spill response, assessment of noise impact on marine mammals and mitigation, and bathymetric mapping.

ALASKA NATIVE COMMUNITIES

The people of Alaska are on the front lines of change. The economic, environmental, and energy choices made as part of U.S. national strategy will affect them for decades to come. Alaska Natives have lived in this harsh region for ten centuries and have successfully adapted to many changes, but the accelerated climate change of the modern era has had a profound impact on indigenous communities in the Arctic.

Amid the search for renewed economic vitality in Alaska, a respect for environmental stewardship and precautionary planning is needed. Infrastructure needs to be developed within the context of sound ecosystem management and understanding of cultural values. Science should also be integrated into infrastructure planning to consider potential climate impact scenarios. For example, when siting a port, it will be essential to know what wildlife migrations and concentrations occur in the area, how the area is needed for subsistence, and how the area is likely to change as a result of climate change.

U.S. strategy in the Arctic needs to acknowledge the stresses within communities in the U.S. Arctic. People in the region face mental and physical health ailments. Water and sanitation are still inadequate for human flourishing in some villages in Alaska. In 2015, the United States committed to the UN Sustainable Development Goals, which includes goal number two on safe water and sanitation. According to the 2014 American Community Survey conducted by the U.S. Census Bureau, 3.8 percent of Alaska households had no plumbing, the highest such rate in the nation. In rural areas, 8 percent "lacked complete plumbing," sixteen times the national level of 0.5 percent.[88] The number of homes in rural Alaska without adequate plumbing is ten times the national average.[89] Reporting on domestic conditions is part of foreign policy. Moreover, a country dedicated to the notion of e pluribus unum (out of many, one) should strive to realize the birthrights of every American, in Kotzebue as well as in Kansas City.

Human security includes food security and basic elements of human well-being. Many Alaska Natives rely on subsistence hunting and gathering, and the changing climate is having an impact on traditional food sources. Social disintegration in parts of Alaska Native communities is evident. Rates of suicide, addiction, and abuse are among the highest in the nation.[90] Yet resilient communities are reclaiming their heritage and trying to plan for the future. Coastal erosion means that some towns will need to relocate. Ironically, some Alaska Natives are in coastal towns only because the federal government forced their nomadic ancestors to settle there. Thus, deciding which and how village residents should move again is emotionally and historically sensitive. Forced displacement interrupts intergenerational knowledge transmission and causes cultural disorientation.

As a country, Americans need to decide how to manage internal climate refugees. From Alaska to Louisiana, people (often poor) are being displaced. The United States may need to deal with a wave of climate refugees as the Arctic continues to warm and rising sea levels flood coastal villages. Although federal support designed for emergency response and rebuilding is available, long-term relocation may require a new office within the Department of Homeland Security. As the situation changes for local communities in the Arctic, the United States will need to broaden its approach to indigenous communities.

Historical and cultural connections across the region have spawned unusual international organizations. Most international organizations are composed solely of states, but the Arctic Council includes six indigenous groups as permanent participants. Although not all people in the Arctic are Inuit, the Inuit Circumpolar Council, which has held special consultative status at the United Nations since 1983, provides an important transborder forum for sharing ideas and highlighting common interests such as the impact of climate change on the food security of subsistence hunters.[91] At the White House Tribal Nations Conference in December 2010, President Obama, in response to calls from Native Americans across the country, announced that the United States would support the nonbinding UN Declaration on the Rights of Indigenous

Peoples, making transborder relations among indigenous Arctic communities a factor in U.S. multilateral diplomacy.[92]

As part of U.S. strategy in the Arctic, policymakers should consider how best to tap Alaska Native expertise to advance policy goals. For instance, playing a role in the Cold War DEW Line provided native communities some sense of purpose and connection to the nation as a whole. Alaska Natives have been observing the region for generations, and including their analyses and observation of climate change could give depth and perspective to policymakers' understanding of the region.[93]

Alaska Native corporations can also play a role. Separate from state-chartered municipal governments and from federally recognized tribal governments, these corporations are unique regional and village structures that share the financial benefits of natural resources among qualified members of Alaska Native descent. Some of these corporations manage significant international investment portfolios; others have more modest assets. Many provide social and cultural services to their members and help form a bridge between traditional communities and the market economy.

FINDINGS AND RECOMMENDATIONS FOR SUPPORTING ALASKA AND ALASKA NATIVE COMMUNITIES

The Task Force finds that

- without an income tax, a corporate tax, or even an agreement to tap its financial reserves, the state of Alaska is ill prepared to offset the reduction in revenue resulting from the decline of oil prices;
- climate change affects Alaska Native locations and livelihoods dramatically;
- subsistence hunters and fishers in the United States rely on their environment directly for food;
- Alaska Natives' concept of food security includes the well-being of the environment;
- a national plan to provide for climate refugees is needed;
- Alaska Natives' expertise can enrich U.S. evaluations of changing conditions in the Arctic;

- drawing on lessons from other countries might be applicable to working with coastal communities in Alaska; and
- given that 3 percent of (and 8 percent of rural) Alaskans lack indoor plumbing, the United States is not fully meeting its commitment to the UN Sustainable Development Goal number two on safe drinking water and sanitation.

The Task Force recommends that

- the U.S. government bolster efforts to improve access to safe drinking water and sanitation in Alaska and throughout the country in accordance with its commitments to the UN Sustainable Development Goals;
- the federal government and state of Alaska work with Alaska Natives to safeguard subsistence hunting, fishing, and gathering; and
- the Department of Homeland Security, in collaboration with that of Health and Human Services, establish an office to coordinate and fund relocation of entire communities when warranted.

Conclusion

The Arctic sits at the crossroads of two major historical trends: the changing climate and the search for better trade routes. The melting of the Arctic sea ice cap opens up possibilities of more navigation as commercial enterprises bring natural resources out of the region and sail across it. Many of the policy recommendations in this report concern technology and infrastructure for safe operation in Arctic conditions. Infrastructure in Alaska—the U.S. Arctic—needs to be strengthened to enable the United States to pursue environmental, economic, and social activity as well as to provide for national security. Throughout history, humanity has sought to move goods down the road or around the world in search of prosperity, ultimately driving trade and shaping world politics. The names Gibraltar, Hormuz, and Malacca are redolent with history, and climate change may soon add the Bering Strait to that list as well. The United States should not only continue, but also augment its renewed focus on the Arctic.

Additional and Dissenting Views

The lack of infrastructure in the U.S. maritime Arctic is a serious national gap with human, security, economic, and environmental implications for the twenty-first century. Many elements of infrastructure mentioned in this report require sustained, long-term investment: hydrography and charting, a viable Arctic port, polar ice-breaking capability, advanced communications, a robust environmental observing system, strengthened monitoring and surveillance, search and rescue capacity, environmental response capacity, aids to navigation, marine salvage, and more. All are necessary to respond to increasing Arctic marine use, facilitate marine navigation, and provide for a robust marine safety and environmental protection framework not only in the U.S. Arctic, but throughout the circumpolar world. From my perspective, two among this long list of needs require immediate federal funding: hydrographic surveying and charting and the revitalization of the U.S. Coast Guard polar ice-breaking fleet.

Increased geodetic and oceanographic observations and expanded hydrography and charting are critical to using the U.S. frontier Arctic maritime region. While there are existing U.S. charts for the entire region, many regions have not been surveyed to modern standards. As indicated in this report, only an estimated 4.7 percent of the U.S. maritime Arctic is charted to modern, international navigation standards. The National Strategy for the Arctic Region issued in May 2013 highlights charting and mapping the Arctic's ocean and waterways as vital to U.S. stewardship and advancing U.S. national interests. Only by increasing the NOAA budget for Arctic hydrography and charting can measurable progress be made. Importantly, the nation's only federal hydrographic ships capable of Arctic survey operations, both commissioned in 1968, require strategic replacement.

The nation's federal polar icebreakers, operated by the U.S. Coast Guard, are instruments of national policy and the visible, sovereign presence of the United States in Arctic and Antarctic waters. They are capital assets that operate, normally independently, in both polar regions, where the United States has broad national interests; they are naval ships as well as the primary U.S. maritime law enforcement presence in polar waters. These multi-mission ships represent a unique polar capability and global reach, undeniably an integral component of American naval and maritime power. The revitalization of these national assets has been the subject of many studies during the past three decades—by interagency groups, independent organizations (including the National Academies of Sciences, Engineering, and Medicine), and the coast guard—and all have affirmed the strategic importance of polar icebreakers operated by the coast guard. None of these comprehensive studies has argued that U.S. national polar maritime interests are served by outsourcing them to foreign governments or commercial interests. Further studies and continued debate about the role of the coast guard icebreaker fleet are unwarranted. Greater clarity on this U.S. strategic requirement has been illuminated by a rapidly changing Arctic and increasing marine use. While the number of new coast guard icebreakers can be debated, these assets are clearly critical for maintaining U.S. global maritime capability, assuring polar marine access, and providing visible and effective U.S. maritime presence, particularly in the U.S. maritime Arctic.

Lawson W. Brigham
joined by Dalee Sambo Dorough, Jill M. Dougherty, and Sherri W. Goodman

It is on the question of how fast the Arctic will open to heavy use, and accordingly in terms of policy urgency, that I disagree with this well-written report. Greater policy urgency is necessary both to tap opportunity and to cope with disaster.

Straight-line extrapolation fails. Acceleration—namely, an incessant, nonlinear increase in temperature, ice melt, transit, resource exploitation, and natural calamity—is likely within the experience of living Americans. For example, with the first credible, commercial success of oil or gas drilling offshore in the Arctic, a gold rush will likely ensue. Within a couple of decades, over four hundred mining and drilling sites will become accessible. The United States must decide whether it wants its firms to be on the forefront of this bonanza or in the wake.

With its symbolic claiming of the North Pole, Russia has already made its intentions clear. It plans to turn its large sector of the Arctic into a Russian lake. Russia already possesses some twenty icebreakers. It is constructing multiple deepwater ports. Because of natural advantages of current and wind, Russia's side of the Arctic is opening first. Russia intends to become the locus of trade and transport from Europe to Asia, out-competing the Panama Canal. China, too, is preparing for a full Arctic role.

Unless the United States wants its coastlines to become a backwater, it likewise must plan for access to industrial sites as well as to cross-Arctic transit along well-marked and charted routes. Deepwater ports are essential.

All of the environmental change is likely to devastate the Arctic. Many populations of caribou, polar bears, walruses, and northern minke whales will be extirpated. Native populations, partially dependent upon these food sources, will suffer hugely. In the lower forty-eight states, from Manhattan to Houston, the rise of water levels will cause devastation to property and life. The problem will be most stark during hurricanes when the storm surge will wipe out large sections of Miami, New Orleans, and Houston, certainly for those thousands of people living in the hundred-year flood plains. Where are the national and local strategies to cope with these virtually inevitable outcomes?

Accompanying all of this crescendo of human activity will be large issues of national security. Transit of the Arctic by the navies of many countries will make Chicago and Toronto the immediate target of cruise missiles and precision-guided bombs.

North America cannot be defended from the Arctic except in terms of close cooperation with Canada. Whatever the internal complications of bureaucratic coordination between commands inside the United States (in practice this has been managed), coordination between countries within NORAD and NORTHCOM is seamless. But the United States and Canada must expand their responsibilities to integrate undersea, surface, air-breathing, and space-based functions within a coordinated whole. Bearing in mind that these joint functions are purely that of monitoring and surveillance, the importance of NORAD and NORTHCOM cannot be exaggerated. Perhaps the greatest indirect consequence of global warming is that it will create new security vulnerabilities in the Arctic that are almost unprecedented.

Charles F. Doran

I fully endorse this report as well as its conclusions and recommendations, especially those concerning indigenous peoples in Alaska. I offer the following information only to elaborate on the significance of the UN Declaration on the Rights of Indigenous Peoples and to offer a broader context for understanding the Sustainable Development Goals (SDGs) from an indigenous perspective.

The UN Declaration is not legally binding in the same manner as treaties, but it has diverse legal effects. It reflects rights already found in human rights treaties, and some of its provisions reflect customary international law.

Since U.S. endorsement in 2010, the declaration has been a consensus international human rights instrument. It has been reaffirmed twice by consensus by the General Assembly. The declaration is regarded as an authoritative source of guidance for diverse institutions, including parliaments, governments, courts, national human rights institutions, and human rights treaty bodies.

States and the General Assembly have recognized, as the UN Commission on Sustainable Development wrote, "the importance of the United Nations Declaration . . . in the context of global, regional, national and subnational implementation of sustainable development strategies." Further, "eradicating poverty in all its forms . . . is . . . an indispensable requirement for sustainable development." In this same context, "the responsibilities of all States . . . to respect, protect, and promote human rights . . . for all, without distinction of any kind" are also emphasized by the United Nations.

It is essential to note that, in addition to the need for safe drinking water and sanitation, the U.S. commitment to other diverse SDGs and SDG Indicators is also important to Arctic indigenous peoples and their cultural integrity, self-reliance, and well-being. The realization of the SDGs by the United States in a spirit of partnership with indigenous peoples must ensure the full exercise and enjoyment of collective and individual human rights. Through self-governance, indigenous peoples must exercise their own responsibilities. These include, inter alia, food and water security, environmental protection, and stewardship of indigenous lands and territories for present and future generations.

Dalee Sambo Dorough

Although I generally agree with the policy recommendations contained in this report, I would like to highlight a difference with one of them. The Task Force, while "recognizing the political obstacles," recommends that the Trump administration make approval of the UN Convention of the Law of the Sea a high priority for its work with the Senate. The Senate should, in my view, provide its advice and consent for UNCLOS ratification, but it has in fact declined to do so for several decades. There is little prospect of this changing in the near term. Because an administration's legislative priority list is limited, and given the array of competing items—including ending sequestration and securing a bipartisan budget deal—it makes little sense to put UNCLOS at the top of the Trump administration's legislative agenda.

Richard H. Fontaine Jr.

Thank you to the many people associated with *Arctic Imperatives* who worked to better understand America's only Arctic state, Alaska, and its people. Alaskan people and the state we inhabit are precious to me, and I desire to continue the dialogue with members of the Task Force and others about these important issues. For that reason, I respectfully submit this dissent.

First, I do not share the view of the report that "by failing to ratify the UNCLOS treaty, the U.S. Senate has undermined the nation's ability to advance its interests in the Arctic to the fullest extent." Substantively and historically, the United States has had and continues to have diplomatic, economic, and military ways to secure all of its interests in the Arctic, whether or not the U.S. Senate ratifies UNCLOS. The president (with Congress) should more clearly define U.S. Arctic interests (as they have already, to some degree, to comply with federal law) and the United States should act as a nation to secure those interests by reasonable means other than UNCLOS.

Second, I believe the Task Force's recommendation that the Trump administration designate an Arctic ambassador reporting to the assistant secretary for the Bureau of Oceans and International Environmental and Scientific Affairs within the U.S. State Department is far too limiting. The Arctic ambassador's portfolio and knowledge base must be far wider than environmental science. Therefore, while working cooperatively with State, the Arctic ambassador could be detailed to a higher level at State, to the president's ambassador to the United Nations, or to the Office of the Vice President.

Third, I disagree with the notion that "for the foreseeable future, most of the threats in the Arctic are derived from resource extraction activities (mining and oil and gas), illegal fishing, search and rescue challenges, and the presence of foreign commercial shipping." Those claims are far too simplistic and also made without the benefit of classified briefings from the Department of Defense or intelligence agencies that would, from my own personal experience, reveal more pressing defense concerns. I do agree, however, that NORTHCOM should be tasked with overall area responsibilities.

Finally, I believe the section on oil and gas is misguided. The report correctly identifies the significant resources in Alaska (billions of barrels and trillions of cubic feet of natural gas available), but effectively argues to leave it in the ground for some undefined time. The Task Force advising on *Arctic Imperatives* is an august body to be sure, but we have no place making the call to lock up U.S. resources—resources that can improve the lives and economic opportunity of all. Rather, the Task Force ought to urge the federal government to follow its own congressionally passed laws, and federal agencies should consistently and timely apply regulations and federal leasing laws. President Obama's ban on Arctic outer continental shelf lease activity should be rescinded. When the federal government more consistently applies and follows the law, more Americans will have opportunity balanced with environmental protection.

Sean Parnell

Endnotes

1. Chris Mooney and Jason Samenow, "The North Pole Is an Insane 36 Degrees Warmer Than Normal as Winter Descends," *Washington Post*, November 17, 2016, http://www.washingtonpost.com/news/energy-environment/wp/2016/11/17/the-north-pole-is-an-insane-36-degrees-warmer-than-normal-as-winter-descends/?utm_term=.70794d57e1cb.
2. Ronald O'Rourke, "Changes in the Arctic: Background and Issues for Congress," CRS Report No. R41153 (Washington, DC: Congressional Research Service, January 5, 2017), p. 1, http://www.fas.org/sgp/crs/misc/R41153.pdf.
3. "Arctic Research and Policy Act of 1984," Public Law 98-373, Sec. 112; U.S. Navy, "U.S. Navy Arctic Roadmap 2014–2030," p. 40.
4. Caitlyn L. Antrim, "The Next Geographical Pivot: The Russian Arctic in the Twenty-First Century," *Naval War College Review*, Summer 2010, pp. 15–37, http://www.usnwc.edu/getattachment/f8217b41-afd2-4649-8378-7b6c8a7e61d2/The-Next-Geographical-Pivot--The-Russian-Arctic-in.aspx.
5. "Quick Facts on Arctic Sea Ice," National Snow and Ice Data Center, https://nsidc.org/cryosphere/quickfacts/seaice.html.
6. Ibid.; "Arctic Ice Shrinks to Second Lowest Level on Record," *New York Times*, September 19, 2016.
7. John E. Walsh, Florence Fetterer, J. Scott Stewart, and William L. Chapman, "A Database for Depicting Arctic Sea Ice Variations Back to 1850," *Geographical Review* Special Issue Arctic 2017, pp. 1–19.
8. Ronald O'Rourke, "Navy Force Structure and Shipbuilding Plans: Background and Issues for Congress," CRS Report No. R32665 (Washington, DC: Congressional Research Service, September 21, 2016), p. 20, http://www.fas.org/sgp/crs/misc/R32665.pdf.
9. George Hale, "NASA Data Peers Into Greenland's Ice Sheet," National Aeronautics and Space Administration, January 23, 2015, http://www.nasa.gov/content/goddard/nasa-data-peers-into-greenlands-ice-sheet.
10. General Accounting Office, *Alaska Native Villages: Limited Progress Has Been Made on Relocating Villages Threatened by Flooding and Erosion*, GAO-09-551, June 3, 2009, http://www.gao.gov/products/GAO-09-551.
11. U.S. Army Corps of Engineers, "Alaska Baseline Erosion Assessment: Study Findings and Technical Report," March 2009, http://climatechange.alaska.gov/docs/iaw_USACE_erosion_rpt.pdf.
12. John Englander, *High Tide on Main Street: Rising Sea Level and the Coming Coastal Crisis*, 2nd ed. (Boca Raton: Science Bookshelf, 2013), p. 107.
13. Forbes Tompkins and Christina Deconcini, "Sea-Level Rise and Its Impact on Miami-Dade County," World Resources Institute Fact Sheet, 2014, http://www.wri.org/sites/default/files/sealevelrise_miami_florida_factsheet_final.pdf.

14. "Under Water: How Sea Level Rise Threatens the Tri-State Region," Regional Plan Association, December 2016, http://www.eenews.net/assets/2016/12/09/document_cw_01.pdf.
15. "Arctic Peoples," Arctic Council, http://www.arctic-council.org/index.php/en/our-work/arctic-peoples; Hugo Ahlenius, "Population Distribution in the Circumpolar Arctic, by Country (Including Indigenous Population)," GRID-Arendal, February 21, 2012, http://www.grida.no/graphicslib/detail/population-distribution-in-the-circumpolar-arctic-by-country-including-indigenous-population_1282.
16. "Arctic Region Policy," The White House, January 9, 2009, http://fas.org/irp/offdocs/nspd/nspd-66.htm.
17. "National Strategy for the Arctic Region," The White House, May 2013, p. 2, https://www.whitehouse.gov/sites/default/files/docs/nat_arctic_strategy.pdf.
18. "Declaration on the Establishment of the Arctic Council," September 19, 1996, https://oaarchive.arctic-council.org/bitstream/handle/11374/85/EDOCS-1752-v2-ACMMCA00_Ottawa_1996_Founding_Declaration.PDF?sequence=5&isAllowed=y.
19. See http://www.arctic-council.org/index.php/en/.
20. "U.S. Chairmanship of the Arctic Council," U.S. Department of State, http://www.state.gov/e/oes/ocns/opa/arc/uschair/.
21. "U.S.-Canada Joint Statement on Climate, Energy, and Arctic Leadership," The White House, March 10, 2016, https://www.whitehouse.gov/the-press-office/2016/03/10/us-canada-joint-statement-climate-energy-and-arctic-leadership.
22. "U.S.-Nordic Leaders' Summit Joint Statement," The White House, May 13, 2016, https://www.whitehouse.gov/the-press-office/2016/05/13/us-nordic-leaders-summit-joint-statement.
23. "United States-Canada Joint Arctic Leaders' Statement," The White House, December 20, 2016, https://www.whitehouse.gov/the-press-office/2016/12/20/united-states-canada-joint-arctic-leaders-statement
24. Ibid.; International Security Advisory Board, "Report on Arctic Policy," U.S. Department of State, September 21, 2016, p. 43, http://www.state.gov/t/avc/isab/262342.html.
25. "Defining the Limits of the U.S. Continental Shelf," U.S. Department of State, http://www.state.gov/e/oes/continentalshelf/.
26. Steven Groves, "Accession to Convention on the Law of the Sea Unnecessary to Advance Arctic Interests," Backgrounder No. 2912, Heritage Foundation, June 26, 2014, http://www.heritage.org/research/reports/2014/06/accession-to-convention-on-the-law-of-the-sea-unnecessary-to-advance-arctic-interests.
27. Supreme Headquarters Allied Powers Europe, "Exercise Cold Response 2016 Wraps Up in Norway," March 9, 2016, https://shape.nato.int/2016/exercise-cold-response-2016-wraps-up-in-norway.
28. Gerard O'Dwyer, "Norway to Reorganize Defense Spending in Response to 'Unpredictable' Russia," *Defense News,* July 1, 2016, http://www.defensenews.com/story/defense/policy-budget/budget/2016/07/01/norway-military-budget-reorganization-armed-forces/86589482/.
29. Rajon Menon and Eugene Rumer, *Conflict in Ukraine: The Unwinding of the Post–Cold War Order* (Cambridge, MA: MIT Press, 2015), pp. 74–75; Matthias Schepp and Gerald Traufetter, "Russia Unveils Aggressive Arctic Plans," *Der Spiegel,* January 29, 2009, http://www.spiegel.de/international/world/riches-at-the-north-pole-russia-unveils-aggressive-arctic-plans-a-604338.html.
30. Heather A. Conley and Caroline Rohloff, "The New Ice Curtain: Russia's Strategic Reach to the Arctic," Center for Strategic and International Studies, August 2015, http://csis-prod.s3.amazonaws.com/s3fs-public/legacy_files/files/publication/150826_Conley_NewIceCurtain_Web.pdf.

31. Marlene Laruelle, *Russia's Arctic Strategies and the Future of the Far North* (Armonk, NY: M. E. Sharpe, 2014), p. 135.
32. International Energy Agency, *Russia 2014: Energy Policies Beyond IEA Countries* (Paris: Organization for Economic Cooperation and Development, 2014), p. 11, https://www.iea.org/publications/freepublications/publication/Russia_2014.pdf.
33. Laruelle, *Russia's Arctic Strategies*, p. 48.
34. Ibid, p. 187.
35. Carlos Barria, "China Wants Ships to Use Faster Arctic Route Opened by Global Warming," *Reuters*, April 20, 2016, http://uk.reuters.com/article/us-china-arctic-idUKKCN0XH08U.
36. Kyle Mizokami, "China Launches a New Icebreaker," *Popular Mechanics*, January 7, 2016, http://www.popularmechanics.com/military/weapons/news/a18867/china-launches-new-icebreaker/.
37. See "NSF and Chinese-Funded Researchers Study Antarctic Bottom-Water Formation," National Science Foundation, https://www.nsf.gov/od/oise/beijing/news_reports/2015-12-17_polar_cooperative_project.pdf.
38. Christopher P. Cavas, "US Navy's New Fleet Goal: 355 Ships," *Defense News*, December 16, 2016, http://www.defensenews.com/articles/us-navys-new-fleet-goal-355-ships.
39. Lawson Brigham, "More Assets for the Arctic," *Proceedings Magazine* 141, no. 12, December 2015, p. 1354.
40. Donald L. Canney, "Icebreakers and the U.S. Coast Guard," U.S. Coast Guard, September 16, 2016, https://www.uscg.mil/history/webcutters/Icebreakers.asp.
41. Ronald O'Rourke, "Coast Guard Polar Icebreaker Modernization: Issues for Congress," CRS Report No. RL34391 (Washington, DC: Congressional Research Service, November 10, 2016), pp. 3–5, https://fas.org/sgp/crs/weapons/RL34391.pdf.
42. "Polar Icebreaker," Acquisition Directorate, U.S. Coast Guard, January 4, 2017, http://www.uscg.mil/acquisition/icebreaker/.
43. "United States Coast Guard High Latitude Region Mission Analysis Capstone Summary," ABS Consulting, July 2010, http://assets.fiercemarkets.net/public/sites/govit/hlssummarycapstone.pdf; O'Rourke, "Coast Guard Polar Icebreaker Modernization."
44. O'Rourke, "Coast Guard Polar Icebreaker Modernization."
45. The Merchant Marine Act of 1920 (Jones Act) regulates coastal marine traffic, requiring that cargo transported between U.S. ports be carried in U.S. vessels. Section 27 notes that such cargo may not be transported in "any other vessel than a vessel built in and documented under the laws of the United States and owned by persons who are citizens of the United States." See John Curtis Perry, Scott Borgerson, and Rockford Weitz, "The Deep Blue Highway," *New York Times*, January 2, 2007, http://www.nytimes.com/2007/01/02/opinion/02perry.html.
46. See "International Code for Ships Operating in Polar Waters," MEPC 68/21/Add. 1 http://www.imo.org/en/MediaCentre/HotTopics/polar/Documents/POLAR%20CODE%20TEXT%20AS%20ADOPTED.pdf.
47. The total U.S. ocean coastline is 12,383 statute miles. The Alaska coastline is 6,640 miles. See "General Coastline and Shoreline of the United States," NOAA Office for Coastal Management, https://coast.noaa.gov/data/docs/states/shorelines.pdf.
48. "Circum-Arctic Resource Appraisal: Estimates of Undiscovered Oil and Gas North of the Arctic Circle," USGS Fact Sheet No. 2008-3049, U.S. Geological Survey, 2008, https://pubs.usgs.gov/fs/2008/3049/fs2008-3049.pdf.
49. David W. Houseknecht, Kenneth J. Bird, and Christopher P. Garrity, "Assessment of Undiscovered Petroleum Resources of the Arctic Alaska Petroleum Province," Scientific Investigations Report 2012-5147 (Reston, VA: U.S. Geological Survey, 2012), p. 1, http://pubs.usgs.gov/sir/2012/5147/pdf/sir2012-5147_arctic.pdf.

50. "Arctic Potential: Realizing the Promise of U.S. Arctic Oil and Gas Resources," National Petroleum Council, March 2015, http://www.npcarcticpotentialreport.org/pdf/AR-Part_1-Final.pdf.
51. "Pipeline Operations," Trans Alaska Pipeline Systems, http://www.alyeska-pipe.com/TAPS/PipelineOperations/LowFlowOperations.
52. Ibid.; "Rankings: Crude Oil Production, September 2016," U.S Energy Information Administration, http://www.eia.gov/state/rankings/?sid=AK#series/46.
53. Clifford Krauss, "U.S. Blocks Arctic Drilling for 2 Years," *New York Times*, October 16, 2015, https://www.nytimes.com/2015/10/17/business/energy-environment/us-blocks-alaskan-arctic-drilling-for-2-years.html.
54. "2017–2022 Lease Sale Schedule," Bureau of Land Management, http://www.boem.gov/2017-2022-Lease-Sale-Schedule/.
55. Elizabeth Harball, "Alaska Native Corporation Acquires Oil and Gas Leases in Arctic Waters," Alaska's Energy Desk, Alaska Public Media, November 17, 2016, http://www.alaskapublic.org/2016/11/17/alaska-native-corporation-acquires-leases-arctic-waters/.
56. Darryl Fears and Juliet Eilperin, "President Obama Bans Oil Drilling in Large Areas of Atlantic and Arctic Oceans," *Washington Post*, December 20, 2016, http://www.washingtonpost.com/news/energy-environment/wp/2016/12/20/president-obama-expected-to-ban-oil-drilling-in-large-areas-of-atlantic-and-arctic-oceans/?utm_term=.334127d6ba43.
57. Kate Ravilious, "Innovation: Methane Capture Gives More Bang for the Buck," *New Scientist*, May 31, 2010, https://www.newscientist.com/article/dn18977-innovation-methane-capture-gives-more-bang-for-the-buck/; Umair Irfan, "Methane Proves Hard to Capture," *Scientific American* reprint of Climatewire, April 23, 2013, http://www.scientificamerican.com/article/methane-proves-hard-to-capture/.
58. As of 2016, the observers at the Arctic Council were China, France, Germany, India, Italy, Japan, the Netherlands, Poland, Republic of Korea, Singapore, Spain, and the United Kingdom.
59. "Zero Routine Flaring by 2030," World Bank, http://www.worldbank.org/en/programs/zero-routine-flaring-by-2030.
60. See Global Agenda Council on the Arctic, "Arctic Investment Protocol: Guidelines for Responsible Investment in the Arctic," World Economic Forum, 2015, http://www3.weforum.org/docs/WEF_Arctic_Investment_Protocol.pdf.
61. "IMO Profile," International Maritime Organization, https://business.un.org/en/entities/13.
62. Barria, "China Wants Ships."
63. Lawson Brigham, Michael Cerne, et al., "Bering Strait Region Case Study," Institute of the North, http://www.institutenorth.org/assets/images/uploads/files/5.5-Bering-Strait-Region-Case-Study.pdf.
64. "Bering Strait," *New World Encyclopedia*, http://www.newworldencyclopedia.org/entry/Bering_Strait.
65. "Executive Order: Northern Bering Sea Climate Resilience," The White House, December 9, 2016, https://www.whitehouse.gov/the-press-office/2016/12/09/executive-order-northern-bering-sea-climate-resilience.
66. "Proposal: Alaska Deep-Draft Arctic Port System Study," City of Nome, September 23, 2015, http://www.usace.army.mil/Portals/2/docs/civilworks/Project%20Planning/wrda/2014/2015_proposals/AK_POD_Alaska_Deep_Draft_Arctic_Port_System_Study_V2.pdf.
67. See 33 USC 2241: Definitions, laws in effect on January 29, 2017, http://uscode.house.gov/view.xhtml?req=(title:33%20section:2241%20edition:prelim).

68. With stations in Canada, Russia, and the United States, the coast guard's long-range radio navigation system provided guidance in the Bering Sea and in Canadian waters. See "LORAN-C General Information: Special Notice Regarding LORAN Closure," U.S. Coast Guard Navigation Center, June 8, 2012, http://www.navcen.uscg.gov/?pageName=loranMain.
69. Tyler Stup, "With WRDA Bill Passed, Nome Arctic Deep Draft Port Back in Conversation," KNOM Mission Radio, September 26, 2016, http://www.ktva.com/with-wrda-bill-passed-nome-arctic-deep-draft-port-back-in-conversation-287/.
70. Arctic Council, *Arctic Marine Shipping Assessment*, 2009, p. 4, http://www.pame.is/images/03_Projects/AMSA/AMSA_2009_report/AMSA_2009_Report_2nd_print.pdf.
71. Ibid., p. 5.
72. Hydrographic Services Review Panel, "Charting the U.S. Maritime Arctic," National Oceanic and Atmospheric Administration, April 2016, http://www.nauticalcharts.noaa.gov/ocs/hsrp/cleveland2016/HSRP-Charting-Maritime-Arctic-22April2016.pdf.
73. "Using New Elevation Data to Explore the Arctic," The White House, September 2, 2015, https://www.whitehouse.gov/blog/2015/09/02/using-new-elevation-data-explore-arctic.
74. CSIS, *New Architecture*, p. 12; Anna B.O. Jensen and Jean-Paul Sicard, "Challenges for Positioning and Navigation in the Arctic," *Coordinates*, October 2010, http://mycoordinates.org/challenges-for-positioning-and-navigation-in-the-arctic/.
75. Jensen and Sicard, "Challenges for Positioning."
76. Arctic Waterways Safety Committee, http://www.arcticwaterways.org/attorneys-1.html.
77. "Rare Earth Elements: What Are They? Who Has Them?" Institute for Energy Research, July 27, 2016, http://instituteforenergyresearch.org/analysis/rare-earth-elements/.
78. Chuin-Wei Yap, "China Ends Rare-Earth Minerals Export Quotas," *Wall Street Journal*, January 5, 2015, http://www.wsj.com/articles/china-ends-rare-earth-minerals-export-quotas-1420441285.
79. "Resource Development Principles in Inuit Nunaat," Inuit Circumpolar Council, June 25, 2014, http://www.inuitcircumpolar.com/resource-development-principles-in-inuit-nunaat.html.
80. "Bering Sea Project," North Pacific Research Board, January 10, 2016, http://www.nprb.org/bering-sea-project/about-the-project/#bsierp_importance.
81. Robert J. Papp, "Statement of Admiral Robert J. Papp, Jr. Special Representative for the Arctic U.S. Department of State Before the Committee on Foreign Affairs, Subcommittees on Europe, Eurasia, and Emerging Threats, and Western Hemisphere," U.S. House of Representatives, November 17, 2015," p. 8, http://docs.house.gov/meetings/FA/FA14/20151117/104201/HHRG-114-FA14-Wstate-PappR-20151117.pdf.
82. Ibid., p. 9.
83. "U.S.-Canada Joint Statement on Climate, Energy, and Arctic Leadership," March 10, 2016.
84. "Rankings: Crude Oil Production, September 2016," U.S. Energy Information Administration, http://www.eia.gov/state/rankings/?sid=AK#series/46.
85. Indian Reorganization Act, 2 U.S.C.A. Section 461 et seq. See also D. Case and D. Voluck, *Alaska Natives and American Laws*, 3rd ed. (Fairbanks: University of Alaska Press, 2012), pp. 98–100.
86. Alaska Native Claims Settlement Act, 18 December 1971, Pub. Law 1, No. 92-203, 85 Stat. 688, 43 U.S.C.A. Sections 1601 et seq. See also Case and Voluck, *Alaska Natives and American Laws*, pp. 165–76.
87. In 2015, the dividend was $2, 072. "Annual Dividend Payment," Alaska Permanent Fund Corporation, http://www.apfc.org/home/Content/dividend/dividendamounts.cfm.

88. High rates of lack of plumbing are also found in pockets of poverty in other parts of the United States. Results of query to Housing Assistance Council, Rural Data Portal Report, "Housing Data, 2013, Alaska Rural and Small Town Areas," November 2, 2016, http://www.ruraldataportal.org/search.aspx.
89. Housing Assistance Council, "Housing in Rural America," p. 46, http://www.ruralhome.org/storage/documents/ts2010/ts-report/ts10_rural_housing.pdf.
90. Sally C. Curtin, Margaret Warner, and Holly Hedegaard, "Suicide Rates for Females and Males by Race and Ethnicity: United States, 1999 and 2014," Centers for Disease Control and Prevention, April 22, 2016, https://www.cdc.gov/nchs/data/hestat/suicide/rates_1999_2014.htm; "Racial and Ethnic Minority Populations," Substance Abuse and Mental Health Service Administration, February 18, 2016, https://www.samhsa.gov/specific-populations/racial-ethnic-minority; Andre B. Rosay, "Violence Against American Indian and Alaska Native Women and Men: 2010 Findings From the National Intimate Partner and Sexual Violence Survey," National Institute of Justice, May 2016, https://www.ncjrs.gov/pdffiles1/nij/249736.pdf.
91. The United Nations Economic and Social Council (ECOSOC) confers special consultative status on non-governmental organizations. See United Nations Economic and Social Council, "List of Non-Governmental Organizations in Consultative Status With the Economic and Social Council as of 1 September 2014," December 4, 2014, E/2014/INF/5, http://csonet.org/content/documents/E-2014-INF-5%20Issued.pdf.
92. "Announcement of U.S. Support for the United Nations Declaration on the Rights of Indigenous Peoples Initiatives to Promote the Government-to-Government Relationship & Improve the Lives of Indigenous Peoples," U.S. Department of State, February 29, 2016, https://2009-2017.state.gov/p/io/humanrights/index.htm.
93. The Inuit Circumpolar Council asserts that "Inuit Traditional Knowledge has provided critical information about climate change impacts in Arctic ecosystems, completing scientific knowledge." The 2016 Arctic Science Ministerial included traditional knowledge. The NSF's EyesNorth community-based observation initiative supports the joint Arctic Council-International Arctic Science Committee program on Sustaining Arctic Observing Networks.

Task Force Members

Task Force members are asked to join a consensus signifying that they endorse "the general policy thrust and judgments reached by the group, though not necessarily every finding and recommendation." They participate in the Task Force in their individual, not their institutional, capacities.

Thad W. Allen retired from the U.S. Coast Guard in 2010, having served as an admiral and as the twenty-third commandant. He currently serves as executive vice president at Booz Allen Hamilton, where he supports government and commercial clients in cybersecurity, energy and the environment, navigation systems, emergency response, and crisis leadership. He is a nationally recognized expert in disaster response and an advisor to government leaders. He was the lead federal official for the responses to Hurricanes Katrina and Rita and the Deepwater Horizon oil spill. He also directed coast guard operations in the wake of the 9/11 attacks and the Haitian earthquake in 2010. A 1971 graduate of the Coast Guard Academy, Allen also holds master's degrees from George Washington University and the Massachusetts Institute of Technology's Sloan School of Management. He is a member of the Council on Foreign Relations and a fellow in the National Academy of Public Administration. He serves on a number of federal advisory committees and holds the James Tyler chair at the Admiral James M. Loy Institute for Leadership at the Coast Guard Academy.

Scott G. Borgerson is the chief executive officer of CargoMetrics Technologies, LLC, a quantitative investment company that trades proprietary maritime data generated from a patented system incorporating advances in data science, scalable computing, and real-time, real-world sensors. A former U.S. Coast Guard officer, Borgerson has held positions as a ship navigator, a patrol boat captain, an assistant professor at the Coast Guard Academy, and the founding managing director of the academy's Admiral James M. Loy Institute for Leadership. Drawing upon his experiences in the coast guard, he cofounded CargoMetrics, a big data company that collects and analyzes hyper accurate data on all ships and cargoes at sea. Prior to founding CargoMetrics in 2009, Borgerson was a fellow at the Council on Foreign Relations. An expert on the Arctic, he has published numerous landmark articles on the region, advises international leaders on emerging Arctic issues, and is a cofounder of the global NGO Arctic Circle. He has testified before a number of congressional committees, contributed to White House strategic policymaking, and his op-eds and articles have appeared in the *Wall Street Journal*, *New York Times*, *Atlantic*, and *Foreign Affairs*.

Lawson W. Brigham is distinguished fellow and faculty member at the International Arctic Research Center at the University of Alaska, Fairbanks (UAF). He is also a fellow at the Coast Guard Academy's Center for Arctic Study and Policy, and senior fellow at the Institute of the North in Anchorage. Brigham was a career coast guard officer and commanded four cutters including the icebreaker *Polar Sea* on Arctic and Antarctic expeditions. From 2004 to 2009 he was chair of the Arctic Council's Arctic marine shipping assessment. Brigham has been a research fellow at Woods Hole Oceanographic Institution; a faculty member of the Coast Guard Academy, the Naval Postgraduate School, and UAF (as distinguished professor of geography and Arctic policy); and Alaska director of the U.S. Arctic Research Commission. He is a graduate of the Coast Guard Academy, a distinguished graduate of the Naval War College, and holds graduate degrees from Rensselaer Polytechnic Institute (MS) and Cambridge University (MPhil and PhD). His research interests have focused on the Russian maritime Arctic, environmental change, polar marine transportation, and polar geopolitics. Brigham is a member of the Council on Foreign Relations, was elected to the Norwegian Scientific Academy for Polar Research, and has been awarded the American Polar Society's Polar Medal.

Esther Brimmer currently serves as the executive director and chief executive officer of NAFSA: Association of International Educators. Brimmer's distinguished career includes three appointments within the U.S. Department of State, serving most recently as the assistant secretary for international organization affairs from April 2009 to 2013.

Prior to joining NAFSA, Brimmer was professor of practice of international affairs at George Washington University's Elliott School of International Affairs, where she served a two-year term as the J.B. and Maurice C. Shapiro professor. She was also an adjunct senior fellow for international institutions at the Council on Foreign Relations and a senior advisor at McLarty Associates. She was previously deputy director and director of research at the Center for Transatlantic Relations at Johns Hopkins University's Paul H. Nitze School of Advanced International Studies (SAIS) from 2001 to 2009 and was a member of the SAIS faculty. She also taught at the College of Europe in Belgium, and from 1995 to 1999 she was a senior associate at the Carnegie Commission on Preventing Deadly Conflict. Earlier, she served on Capitol Hill as a legislative analyst for the Democratic Study Group in the U.S. House of Representatives. Immediately after earning her PhD from Oxford University, she spent two years as a management consultant with McKinsey & Company.

Stephen A. Cheney is the chief executive officer (CEO) of the American Security Project. He is a graduate of the U.S. Naval Academy and has over thirty years' experience as a marine. His primary specialty was artillery, but he focused extensively on entry-level training and commanded at every echelon at both Marine Corps Recruit Depots, including as the commanding general at Parris Island. He served several years in Japan and has traveled extensively throughout the Middle East and Asia. Other selected highlights of his military career include tours as deputy executive secretary to defense secretaries Dick Cheney and Les Aspin, ground plans officer for drug enforcement policy in the Pentagon, liaison to the congressional commission on roles and missions of the armed forces, and inspector general of the U.S. Marine Corps. Following retirement from the marines, he became the chief operating officer for Business Executives for National Security in Washington, DC, and most recently was president and CEO of the Marine Military Academy in Harlingen, Texas. A graduate of the Marine Corps Command and Staff College and the National War College, he has an MS from the University of Southern California. He was a military fellow at the Council on Foreign Relations, where he is a member. He was appointed to the secretary of state's international security advisory board in December 2013, and more recently to the foreign affairs policy board.

Charles F. Doran is the Andrew W. Mellon professor of international relations at Johns Hopkins University's Paul H. Nitze School of Advanced International Studies. There he serves both as director of the global theory and history program and as director of the program on Canadian studies. Doran has written widely on trade matters, environmental protection, oil economics and politics, and security. He has provided briefings and testimony on energy and environmental matters, trade policy, and international security before committees of the U.S. Congress and the Canadian Parliament. An entire issue of the *International Political Science Review* was devoted to his work on structural change and security in world politics. He is currently working on a book that assesses world order in the twenty-first century. Doran has received the Governor General's International Award in Canadian Studies, the highest scholarly award in the field. The American Political Science Association bestowed on him its Mildred A. Schwartz Lifetime Achievement Award in Canadian studies. For his contributions in international relations, the International Studies Association granted him its Foreign Policy Analysis Distinguished Scholar Award.

Dalee Sambo Dorough (Inuit-Alaska), specializes in public international law, international relations, indigenous human rights standards, and the status and rights of Arctic indigenous peoples. A former chairperson and expert member of the UN Permanent Forum on Indigenous Issues (PFII), she is an associate professor at University of Alaska, Anchorage, with an appointment at the Institute for Social and Economic Research. Since 1984, she has participated in the work of the United Nations, International Labor Organization, Organization of American States, and other international forums concerning the human rights of indigenous peoples. Recent publications include "The Rights, Interests and Role of the Arctic Council Permanent Participants" chapter in *Governance of Arctic Shipping: Balancing Rights and Interests of Arctic States and User States* and a UN PFII study on how states exploit weak procedural rules in international organizations to devalue the UN Declaration on the Rights of Indigenous Peoples and other international human rights law. She holds a master of arts in law and diplomacy from Tufts University's Fletcher School of Law and Diplomacy and a PhD from the University of British Columbia's Peter A. Allard School of Law.

Jill M. Dougherty served as a CNN correspondent for three decades, reporting from more than fifty countries. Her area of expertise is Russia and the post-Soviet region. She is currently a global fellow at the Woodrow Wilson International Center for Scholars in Washington, DC; a CNN contributor, providing expert commentary on Russia; and a distinguished visiting practitioner at the Evans School of Public Policy and Governance at the University of Washington, Seattle. In 2014, Dougherty was selected as a fellow at the Harvard Kennedy School's Shorenstein Center on Media, Politics, and Public Policy, where she studied the Russian government's international and domestic media strategy. She conducted additional research as a public policy scholar at the Wilson Center and at the International Centre for Defense and Security in Tallinn, Estonia. Dougherty joined CNN in 1983 and served as CNN's Moscow bureau chief from 1997 to 2005 and as CNN White House correspondent from 1991 to 1996. She also served as CNN's foreign affairs correspondent, based in Washington, DC; U.S. affairs editor for CNN International; and CNN International's managing editor for the Asia-Pacific region, based in Hong Kong. She has a BA in Slavic languages and literature from the University of Michigan, a certificate of study from Leningrad State University, and a master's degree from Georgetown University.

Richard H. Fontaine Jr. is the president of the Center for a New American Security (CNAS). He is also an adjunct professor in the security studies program at Georgetown University's School of Foreign Service. He previously served at CNAS as a senior fellow, and he was a foreign policy advisor to Senator John McCain (R-AZ) for more than five years. He has also worked at the State Department, the National Security Council (NSC), and on the staff of the Senate Committee on Foreign Relations. Fontaine served as foreign policy advisor to the McCain 2008 presidential campaign and, following the election, as the minority deputy staff director on the Senate Armed Services Committee. Before that, he served as associate director for Near Eastern affairs at the NSC and worked in the NSC's Asian affairs directorate. During his time at the State Department, Fontaine worked in the office of former Deputy Secretary of State Richard Armitage and in the South Asia bureau. He began his foreign policy career as a staff member of the Senate Committee on Foreign Relations, focusing on the Middle East and South Asia. Fontaine graduated from Tulane University and Johns Hopkins

University's School of Advanced International Studies, and he attended Oxford University.

Sherri W. Goodman is an executive, lawyer, and a former defense official and Senate Armed Services Committee staff professional. She is currently a senior fellow at both CNA and the Woodrow Wilson International Center for Scholars. She has served as the president and chief executive officer of the Consortium for Ocean Leadership, which manages ocean science and technology programs on behalf of oceanographic research institutions. Goodman previously served as senior vice president and general counsel of CNA. She is the founder and executive director of the CNA military advisory board, whose landmark reports include *National Security and the Threat of Climate Change* and *National Security and the Accelerating Risks of Climate Change*. Goodman served as the first deputy undersecretary of defense for environmental security and has twice received the Department of Defense medal for distinguished public service. Goodman is a member of the secretary of state's international security advisory board. She serves on the boards of the Atlantic Council, Committee on Conscience of the U.S. Holocaust Museum, the Joint Ocean Commission leadership initiative, the Marshall Legacy Institute, the University Corporation for Atmospheric Research, and the U.S. Water Partnership. She is a member of the Council on Foreign Relations. A graduate of Amherst College, she has degrees from Harvard Law School and the Harvard Kennedy School.

Katherine A. Hardin is a senior director with IHS Markit. Previously, Hardin has led IHS Cambridge Energy Research Associates' Russian and Caspian energy team and IHS institutional investor energy research. She is currently the commercial director for IHS analysis on climate and carbon and is overseeing an IHS study on the transition to electric vehicles. Hardin's own research area focuses on energy development in the Arctic, Russia, and Central Asia, and she has written widely on oil and gas production and export routes from Russia and the Caspian region. Hardin has worked extensively in Russia and the former Soviet Union since 1990. Prior to joining IHS, Hardin was an energy consultant with PricewaterhouseCoopers, advising on power sector privatization throughout Russia and the Caspian region. Hardin is a member of the Council on Foreign Relations, a fellow with the United

States-Japan Foundation, and a member of the Arctic Deeply advisory board. She graduated Phi Beta Kappa from Wesleyan University and holds an MA from Yale University and an MBA from the Yale School of Management.

Jane Lubchenco, university distinguished professor at Oregon State University, is a marine ecologist with expertise in the ocean, climate change, and interactions between the environment and human well-being. She served as undersecretary of commerce for oceans and atmosphere, administrator of the National Oceanic and Atmospheric Administration, and as part of President Obama's science team from 2009 to 2013. She was also the first U.S. science envoy for the ocean, a pro bono position with the State Department, from 2014 to 2016. Lubchenco is one of the most highly cited ecologists in the world, and eight of her publications are considered science citation classics. She is a member of the National Academy of Sciences among other distinguished academies and has received numerous awards, including twenty honorary doctorates and the highest honor given by the National Academy of Sciences, the Public Welfare Medal. Lubchenco cofounded three organizations that train scientists to be better communicators and engage more effectively with the public, policymakers, media, and industry: the Leopold Leadership Program, COMPASS, and Climate Central. She is passionate about scientists communicating with citizens to create knowledge and craft durable solutions to enable vibrant communities, strong economies, and a healthy planet. She holds a PhD in ecology from Harvard University.

Kimberly Marten is the Ann Whitney Olin professor of political science at Barnard College, Columbia University, and the director of the program on U.S.-Russia relations at Columbia's Harriman Institute. She has written four books, most recently *Warlords: Strong-Arm Brokers in Weak States*. Her first book, *Engaging the Enemy: Organization Theory and Soviet Military Innovation*, won the Marshall D. Shulman Book Prize. She has written academic articles for *Armed Forces and Society*, *International Peacekeeping*, *International Security*, *Journal of Intervention and Statebuilding*, *Journal of Slavic Military Studies*, *Post-Soviet Affairs*, and *Problems of Post-Communism*, and her policy articles have appeared in the *Washington Quarterly*, ForeignAffairs.com, *Washington Post*'s Monkey Cage blog, and *Huffington Post*, among others. She is a frequent media commentator and appeared on *The Daily Show* with Jon Stewart to discuss Vladimir Putin and Russia. She is a member of the Council on Foreign Relations.

Marvin E. Odum recently retired as the chairman and president of Shell Oil Company and executive committee director for Royal Dutch Shell plc, a role he had held since 2009. He joined Shell as an engineer in 1982 and held a variety of management positions in technical and commercial operations across multiple business areas, including executive vice president for exploration and productions in the Americas and director of Americas Shell Gas and Power. Odum also spent time in the global power generation business as chief executive officer of InterGen from 2004 to 2005. He served on the American Petroleum Institute executive committee and board from 2008 to 2016. He is a member of the Council on Foreign Relations, board member of the National Urban League, dean's council member of the Harvard Kennedy School, engineering advisory board member for the University of Texas, and board of visitors member of both the University of Houston and the MD Anderson Cancer Center. He earned a BS in mechanical engineering from the University of Texas and an MBA from the University of Houston.

Sean Parnell served as the governor of Alaska from 2009 to 2014 and as Alaska's lieutenant governor from 2006 to 2009. During his tenure as governor, Parnell designed and led implementation of public policies for America's only Arctic state with the goal of creating opportunity for Alaskans. Under Parnell's leadership, Alaska experienced an economic turnaround with billions of new dollars flowing into private sector investments and a record-setting level of employment and job creation in Alaska. Parnell also led the way to greater safety and dignity by fighting domestic violence, sexual assault, and human trafficking through the creation of Choose Respect, a comprehensive initiative focused on prevention, intervention, and support services for victims and survivors. Additionally, Parnell created educational opportunity for thousands of young Alaskans by creating the Alaska Performance Scholarship, a merit scholarship for university and job training programs that every young Alaskan can earn by successfully completing additional high school course work. The former governor has practiced law for two decades and is licensed to practice in Alaska and Washington, DC. Parnell and Alaska's former first lady, Sandy Parnell, have been married twenty-nine years and continue to live and work in Alaska.

James B. Steinberg is university professor of social science, international affairs, and law at Syracuse University, where he was dean of the Maxwell School of Citizenship and Public Affairs from July 2011 until June 2016. Prior to becoming dean he served as deputy secretary of state, the principal deputy to Secretary Hillary Clinton. From 2005 to 2008 Steinberg was dean of the Lyndon B. Johnson School of Public Affairs at the University of Texas, Austin. From 2001 to 2005, Steinberg was vice president and director of foreign policy studies at the Brookings Institution. Steinberg was deputy national security advisor to President Bill Clinton from 1996 to 2000, and during that period he also served as the president's personal representative to the 1998 and 1999 Group of Eight (G8) summits. Prior to becoming deputy national security advisor, Steinberg held positions as director of the State Department's policy planning staff and as deputy assistant secretary for analysis in the Bureau of Intelligence and Research. He is the recipient of the American Political Science Association's Joseph J. Kruzel Memorial Award for Public Service, the Central Intelligence Agency's Director's Medal, and the Secretary of State's Distinguished Service Award.

Rockford Weitz is professor of practice and director of the maritime studies program at Tufts University's Fletcher School of Law and Diplomacy, where he teaches courses on global maritime affairs, maritime security, and entrepreneurial leadership. He also serves as president of the Institute for Global Maritime Studies, a nonprofit that seeks practical solutions to global maritime challenges, and as president and CEO at Rhumb Line, LLC, a consultancy that provides strategic advice to entrepreneurs and startups. A serial entrepreneur, Weitz served as founding executive director at FinTech Sandbox, founding CEO at CargoMetrics, and international counsel at Schweitzer Engineering Laboratories, Inc. He also worked at the Office of the U.S. Trade Representative and served as founding program director of the Borgenicht Peace Initiative. He serves on the board of directors at several nonprofits, including Blue Water Metrics and the Commonwealth Children's Center. Weitz has published op-eds in the *New York Times, Christian Science Monitor*, and *Straits Times* (Singapore), among others. He earned a BA in international relations and political economy from the College of William and Mary, a JD from Harvard Law School, and an MA and PhD from the Fletcher School.

Christine Todd Whitman is president of the Whitman Strategy Group (WSG), a consulting firm that specializes in energy and environmental issues. WSG offers a comprehensive set of solutions to problems facing businesses, organizations, and governments; it has been at the forefront of helping leading companies find innovative solutions to environmental challenges. Whitman served in the cabinet of President George W. Bush as administrator of the Environmental Protection Agency from January 2001 until June 2003. She was the fiftieth governor of the State of New Jersey, serving as its first woman governor from 1994 until 2001. She is the author of the *New York Times* best seller *It's My Party Too: The Battle for the Heart of the GOP and the Future of America*, which was published in January 2005 and released in paperback in March 2006. Whitman serves on the board of directors of Texas Instruments, Inc., and United Technologies Corporation, and formerly served on the board of SC Johnson and Son, Inc. She is a member of the Nuclear Matters advisory council and Terrestrial Energy's international advisory board. She holds an executive masters professional director certification from the American College of Corporate Directors. Whitman also serves a number of nonprofit organizations, including as chairman of the American Security Project and vice-chairman of the trustees of the Eisenhower Fellowships. She is a member of the board of directors of the Center for Responsible Shale Development. She co-chairs the Joint Ocean Commission initiative leadership council and is on the advisory board of the Corporate Eco Forum.

Margaret D. Williams is managing director of World Wildlife Fund's U.S. Arctic field program, which entails leading a team of experts in climate change, wildlife biology, fisheries, oil and shipping, and communications to implement an international conservation strategy for the Bering, Chukchi, and Beaufort Seas. Williams has a special interest in Russian conservation. She speaks Russian, and was founder and editor for twelve years of the quarterly journal *Russian Conservation News.* Before joining the World Wildlife Fund in 1997, she worked as a consultant to the World Bank on biodiversity projects in Russia and Central Asia. Williams is currently a member of the board of the Alaska Ocean Observing System, and the advisory board of the University of Alaska's College of Fisheries and Ocean Sciences. She is a member of the Council on Foreign Relations. Williams received a bachelor's degree in American studies from Smith College and a master's degree from Yale University's School of Forestry and Environmental Studies.

Kenneth S. Yalowitz became the director of the conflict resolution MA program at Georgetown University on July 1, 2015. He is also a global fellow at the Woodrow Wilson International Center for Scholars in Washington, DC. He previously served as the director of Dartmouth College's John Sloan Dickey Center for International Understanding from 2003 to 2011, following retirement from the U.S. Department of State after thirty-six years as a career diplomat and member of the Senior Foreign Service. He served as a U.S. ambassador to Belarus from 1994 to 1997 and to Georgia from 1998 to 2001. Other overseas assignments included Moscow (twice), The Hague, and the U.S. Mission to NATO in Brussels. He won a variety of awards for conflict prevention and overall diplomatic performance. Yalowitz was chosen for the Ambassador Robert Frasure award for peacemaking and conflict prevention in 2000 for his work to prevent the spillover of the Chechen war into Georgia. In 2009 he joined the American Academy of Diplomacy, and in 2011 became a member of the Council on Foreign Relations.

Task Force Observers

Observers participate in Task Force discussions, but are not asked to join the consensus. They participate in their individual, not institutional, capacities.

John B. Bellinger III is adjunct senior fellow for international and national security law at the Council on Foreign Relations. He is also a partner in the international and national security practices at Arnold & Porter Kaye Scholer LLP in Washington, DC. From 2005 to 2009, Bellinger was the legal advisor for the Department of State, where he was the principal international lawyer for the U.S. government and directed the Office of the Legal Advisor. Bellinger served from 2001 to 2005 as senior associate counsel to the president and legal advisor to the National Security Council at the White House. He previously served as counsel for national security matters in the criminal division of the Justice Department during the Clinton administration, as special counsel to the Senate Select Committee on Intelligence, and as special assistant to Director of Central Intelligence William H. Webster. Bellinger is one of four U.S. members of the Permanent Court of Arbitration in The Hague, which nominates judges to the International Court of Justice. His op-eds on international law have appeared in the *New York Times*, *Washington Post*, *Wall Street Journal*, and *International Herald Tribune*. Bellinger received his AB from Princeton in 1982, his JD from Harvard Law School in 1986, and an MA in foreign affairs from the University of Virginia in 1991.

Colonel Brian R. Bruckbauer is currently a senior U.S. Air Force fellow at the Council on Foreign Relations. Previously, he commanded Joint Base Elmendorf-Richardson and the 673rd Air Base Wing in Alaska, where he was responsible for 5,500 personnel, $11.4 billion in infrastructure, and support to over 35,000 people throughout Alaska.

Previously, he served as the military assistant to the undersecretary of defense for policy, as well as numerous other command, staff, and deployed positions. He received a BA from the University of St. Thomas in St. Paul, Minnesota, an MA from George Washington University, and an MS from the National War College.

Walter A. Berbrick is an international affairs fellow at the Council on Foreign Relations and senior advisor to the special representative for the Arctic at the State Department. He is on sabbatical from the Naval War College, where he serves as an associate professor in the war gaming department and founding director of the Arctic Studies Group (ASG). Under his leadership, the ASG serves as a focal point, stimulus, and major source of strategic and operational thought on U.S. Arctic policy and military strategy within the navy, joint, and interagency communities. Berbrick previously served as an intelligence officer in the navy and taught undergraduate and graduate courses at Saint Peter's University and Salve Regina University. He is a member of the Arctic security working group at Stanford's Hoover Institution and is currently working on an edited volume on international security and defense in the Arctic region. Berbrick holds a BA in criminal justice from Saint Peter's University, MA in international relations from Salve Regina University, MA in national security and strategic studies from the Naval War College, and doctorate in law and policy from Northeastern University.

Captain Ron LaBrec is a U.S. Coast Guard officer specializing in maritime security, crisis management and communication, and talent management. He serves as assistant superintendent of the Coast Guard Academy and was a 2015–2016 visiting fellow at the Council on Foreign Relations. LaBrec has served in operational and management roles at sea and ashore including commanding the Coast Guard Recruiting Command, where he led recruiters in attracting, inspiring, and hiring the service's workforce. He previously directed the U.S. Coast Guard office of public affairs, overseeing the service's media, digital, and corporate communications, as well as its community relations and history programs. He has directed external communications for high profile events such as responses to the BP Deepwater Horizon oil spill, Hurricane Katrina, and the 9/11 terrorist attacks, as well as coast guard rescue and security operations. LaBrec has a bachelor's degree in government from the Coast Guard Academy and a master's degree in public relations from Boston University. He is an alumnus of the Massachusetts Institute of Technology's Seminar XXI program in national security and international relations, as well as the Aspen Institute's executive leadership seminar.

Lieutenant Commander Amy McElroy is a U.S. Coast Guard fellow in the office of Senator Lisa Murkowski (R-AK), working on Arctic, oceans, marine transportation, Department of Homeland Security, science, and technology issues. She enlisted in the coast guard in 2001 and served as a quartermaster on the coast guard cutters *Sweetgum* and *Cypress*. McElroy received her officer's commission in 2003 and has been stationed in Mobile, Alabama; Port Arthur, Texas; and Washington, DC. She has spent her career in marine safety conducting oil spill and disaster response and commercial vessel inspections. She holds a BS in biology from the University of North Texas and a master's of public service and administration from Texas A&M University's Bush School of Government and Public Service.

Anya Schmemann (observer, ex officio) is Washington director of Global Communications and Outreach and director of the Independent Task Force Program at the Council on Foreign Relations in Washington, DC. She recently served as assistant dean of communications and outreach at American University's School of International Service. Previously, Schmemann managed communications at the Harvard Kennedy School's Belfer Center for Science and International Affairs and administered the Caspian studies program there. She coordinated a research project on Russian security issues at the EastWest Institute in New York and was assistant director of CFR's Center for Preventive Action in New York, focusing on the Balkans and Central Asia. She received a BA in government and an MA in Russian, East European, and Central Asian studies, both from Harvard University. She was a Truman national security fellow, a nonresident senior fellow at the Center for the National Interest, and was a term member and is now a life member of the Council on Foreign Relations.

Stephen Sestanovich is the George F. Kennan senior fellow for Russian and Eurasian studies at the Council on Foreign Relations and the Kathryn and Shelby Cullom Davis professor of international diplomacy at Columbia University's School of International and

Public Affairs. He is the author of *Maximalist: America in the World from Truman to Obama*. From 1997 to 2001, Sestanovich was the State Department's ambassador-at-large for the former Soviet Union. He previously served as vice president for Russian and Eurasian affairs at the Carnegie Endowment for International Peace, director of Soviet and East European studies at the Center for Strategic and International Studies, senior director for policy development at the National Security Council, a member of the State Department's policy planning staff, and senior legislative assistant to the late Senator Daniel Patrick Moynihan (D-NY). Sestanovich comments frequently on international issues for radio and television and has written for major newspapers, magazines, and other publications. He is a member of the board of directors of the National Endowment for Democracy. He received his BA summa cum laude from Cornell University and his PhD from Harvard University.

Kate Wolgemuth serves as a legislative assistant in the office of Senator Dan Sullivan (R-AK), working on Arctic, Indian affairs, agriculture, health, and housing issues. Prior to her work in the Senate, she served as an associate director of state and federal relations for former Alaska Governor Sean Parnell and current Governor Bill Walker. She holds a bachelor of arts in history and political science from Colgate University.

Independent Task Force Reports

Published by the Council on Foreign Relations

A Sharper Choice on North Korea: Engaging China for a Stable Northeast Asia
Mike Mullen and Sam Nunn, Chairs; Adam Mount, Project Director
Independent Task Force Report No. 74 (2016)

Working With a Rising India: A Joint Venture for the New Century
Charles R. Kaye and Joseph S. Nye Jr., Chairs; Alyssa Ayres, Project Director
Independent Task Force Report No. 73 (2015)

The Emerging Global Health Crisis: Noncommunicable Diseases in Low- and Middle-Income Countries
Mitchell E. Daniels Jr. and Thomas E. Donilon, Chairs; Thomas J. Bollyky, Project Director
Independent Task Force Report No. 72 (2014)

North America: Time for a New Focus
David H. Petraeus and Robert B. Zoellick, Chairs; Shannon K. O'Neil, Project Director
Independent Task Force No. 71 (2014)

Defending an Open, Global, Secure, and Resilient Internet
John D. Negroponte and Samuel J. Palmisano, Chairs; Adam Segal, Project Director
Independent Task Force Report No. 70 (2013)

U.S.-Turkey Relations: A New Partnership
Madeleine K. Albright and Stephen J. Hadley, Chairs; Steven A. Cook, Project Director
Independent Task Force Report No. 69 (2012)

U.S. Education Reform and National Security
Joel I. Klein and Condoleezza Rice, Chairs; Julia Levy, Project Director
Independent Task Force Report No. 68 (2012)

U.S. Trade and Investment Policy
Andrew H. Card and Thomas A. Daschle, Chairs; Edward Alden and Matthew J. Slaughter, Project Directors
Independent Task Force Report No. 67 (2011)

Global Brazil and U.S.-Brazil Relations
Samuel W. Bodman and James D. Wolfensohn, Chairs; Julia E. Sweig, Project Director
Independent Task Force Report No. 66 (2011)

U.S. Strategy for Pakistan and Afghanistan
Richard L. Armitage and Samuel R. Berger, Chairs; Daniel S. Markey, Project Director
Independent Task Force Report No. 65 (2010)

U.S. Policy Toward the Korean Peninsula
Charles L. Pritchard and John H. Tilelli Jr., Chairs; Scott A. Snyder, Project Director
Independent Task Force Report No. 64 (2010)

U.S. Immigration Policy
Jeb Bush and Thomas F. McLarty III, Chairs; Edward Alden, Project Director
Independent Task Force Report No. 63 (2009)

U.S. Nuclear Weapons Policy
William J. Perry and Brent Scowcroft, Chairs; Charles D. Ferguson, Project Director
Independent Task Force Report No. 62 (2009)

Confronting Climate Change: A Strategy for U.S. Foreign Policy
George E. Pataki and Thomas J. Vilsack, Chairs; Michael A. Levi, Project Director
Independent Task Force Report No. 61 (2008)

U.S.-Latin America Relations: A New Direction for a New Reality
Charlene Barshefsky and James T. Hill, Chairs; Shannon O'Neil, Project Director
Independent Task Force Report No. 60 (2008)

U.S.-China Relations: An Affirmative Agenda, A Responsible Course
Carla A. Hills and Dennis C. Blair, Chairs; Frank Sampson Jannuzi, Project Director
Independent Task Force Report No. 59 (2007)

National Security Consequences of U.S. Oil Dependency
John Deutch and James R. Schlesinger, Chairs; David G. Victor, Project Director
Independent Task Force Report No. 58 (2006)

Russia's Wrong Direction: What the United States Can and Should Do
John Edwards and Jack Kemp, Chairs; Stephen Sestanovich, Project Director
Independent Task Force Report No. 57 (2006)

More than Humanitarianism: A Strategic U.S. Approach Toward Africa
Anthony Lake and Christine Todd Whitman, Chairs; Princeton N. Lyman and J. Stephen Morrison, Project Directors
Independent Task Force Report No. 56 (2006)

In the Wake of War: Improving Post-Conflict Capabilities
Samuel R. Berger and Brent Scowcroft, Chairs; William L. Nash, Project Director; Mona K. Sutphen, Deputy Director
Independent Task Force Report No. 55 (2005)

In Support of Arab Democracy: Why and How
Madeleine K. Albright and Vin Weber, Chairs; Steven A. Cook, Project Director
Independent Task Force Report No. 54 (2005)

Building a North American Community
John P. Manley, Pedro Aspe, and William F. Weld, Chairs; Thomas d'Aquino, Andrés Rozental, and Robert Pastor, Vice Chairs; Chappell H. Lawson, Project Director
Independent Task Force Report No. 53 (2005)

Iran: Time for a New Approach
Zbigniew Brzezinski and Robert M. Gates, Chairs; Suzanne Maloney, Project Director
Independent Task Force Report No. 52 (2004)

An Update on the Global Campaign Against Terrorist Financing
Maurice R. Greenberg, Chair; William F. Wechsler and Lee S. Wolosky, Project Directors
Independent Task Force Report No. 40B (Web-only release, 2004)

Renewing the Atlantic Partnership
Henry A. Kissinger and Lawrence H. Summers, Chairs; Charles A. Kupchan, Project Director
Independent Task Force Report No. 51 (2004)

Iraq: One Year After
Thomas R. Pickering and James R. Schlesinger, Chairs; Eric P. Schwartz, Project Consultant
Independent Task Force Report No. 43C (Web-only release, 2004)

Nonlethal Weapons and Capabilities
Paul X. Kelley and Graham Allison, Chairs; Richard L. Garwin, Project Director
Independent Task Force Report No. 50 (2004)

New Priorities in South Asia: U.S. Policy Toward India, Pakistan, and Afghanistan (Chairmen's Report)
Marshall Bouton, Nicholas Platt, and Frank G. Wisner, Chairs; Dennis Kux and Mahnaz Ispahani, Project Directors
Independent Task Force Report No. 49 (2003)
Cosponsored with the Asia Society

Finding America's Voice: A Strategy for Reinvigorating U.S. Public Diplomacy
Peter G. Peterson, Chair; Kathy Bloomgarden, Henry Grunwald, David E. Morey, and Shibley Telhami, Working Committee Chairs; Jennifer Sieg, Project Director; Sharon Herbstman, Project Coordinator
Independent Task Force Report No. 48 (2003)

Emergency Responders: Drastically Underfunded, Dangerously Unprepared
Warren B. Rudman, Chair; Richard A. Clarke, Senior Adviser; Jamie F. Metzl, Project Director
Independent Task Force Report No. 47 (2003)

Iraq: The Day After (Chairs' Update)
Thomas R. Pickering and James R. Schlesinger, Chairs; Eric P. Schwartz, Project Director
Independent Task Force Report No. 43B (Web-only release, 2003)

Burma: Time for Change
Mathea Falco, Chair
Independent Task Force Report No. 46 (2003)

Afghanistan: Are We Losing the Peace?
Marshall Bouton, Nicholas Platt, and Frank G. Wisner, Chairs; Dennis Kux and Mahnaz Ispahani, Project Directors
Chairman's Report of an Independent Task Force (2003)
Cosponsored with the Asia Society

Meeting the North Korean Nuclear Challenge
Morton I. Abramowitz and James T. Laney, Chairs; Eric Heginbotham, Project Director
Independent Task Force Report No. 45 (2003)

Chinese Military Power
Harold Brown, Chair; Joseph W. Prueher, Vice Chair; Adam Segal, Project Director
Independent Task Force Report No. 44 (2003)

Iraq: The Day After
Thomas R. Pickering and James R. Schlesinger, Chairs; Eric P. Schwartz, Project Director
Independent Task Force Report No. 43 (2003)

Threats to Democracy: Prevention and Response
Madeleine K. Albright and Bronislaw Geremek, Chairs; Morton H. Halperin, Director; Elizabeth Frawley Bagley, Associate Director
Independent Task Force Report No. 42 (2002)

America—Still Unprepared, Still in Danger
Gary Hart and Warren B. Rudman, Chairs; Stephen E. Flynn, Project Director
Independent Task Force Report No. 41 (2002)

Terrorist Financing
Maurice R. Greenberg, Chair; William F. Wechsler and Lee S. Wolosky, Project Directors
Independent Task Force Report No. 40 (2002)

Enhancing U.S. Leadership at the United Nations
David Dreier and Lee H. Hamilton, Chairs; Lee Feinstein and Adrian Karatnycky, Project Directors
Independent Task Force Report No. 39 (2002)
Cosponsored with Freedom House

Improving the U.S. Public Diplomacy Campaign in the War Against Terrorism
Carla A. Hills and Richard C. Holbrooke, Chairs; Charles G. Boyd, Project Director
Independent Task Force Report No. 38 (Web-only release, 2001)

Building Support for More Open Trade
Kenneth M. Duberstein and Robert E. Rubin, Chairs; Timothy F. Geithner, Project Director; Daniel R. Lucich, Deputy Project Director
Independent Task Force Report No. 37 (2001)

Beginning the Journey: China, the United States, and the WTO
Robert D. Hormats, Chair; Elizabeth Economy and Kevin Nealer, Project Directors
Independent Task Force Report No. 36 (2001)

Strategic Energy Policy Update
Edward L. Morse, Chair; Amy Myers Jaffe, Project Director
Independent Task Force Report No. 33B (2001)
Cosponsored with the James A. Baker III Institute for Public Policy of Rice University

Testing North Korea: The Next Stage in U.S. and ROK Policy
Morton I. Abramowitz and James T. Laney, Chairs; Robert A. Manning, Project Director
Independent Task Force Report No. 35 (2001)

The United States and Southeast Asia: A Policy Agenda for the New Administration
J. Robert Kerrey, Chair; Robert A. Manning, Project Director
Independent Task Force Report No. 34 (2001)

Strategic Energy Policy: Challenges for the 21st Century
Edward L. Morse, Chair; Amy Myers Jaffe, Project Director
Independent Task Force Report No. 33 (2001)
Cosponsored with the James A. Baker III Institute for Public Policy of Rice University

A Letter to the President and a Memorandum on U.S. Policy Toward Brazil
Stephen Robert, Chair; Kenneth Maxwell, Project Director
Independent Task Force Report No. 32 (2001)

State Department Reform
Frank C. Carlucci, Chair; Ian J. Brzezinski, Project Coordinator
Independent Task Force Report No. 31 (2001)
Cosponsored with the Center for Strategic and International Studies

U.S.-Cuban Relations in the 21st Century: A Follow-on Report
Bernard W. Aronson and William D. Rogers, Chairs; Julia Sweig and Walter Mead, Project Directors
Independent Task Force Report No. 30 (2000)

Toward Greater Peace and Security in Colombia: Forging a Constructive U.S. Policy
Bob Graham and Brent Scowcroft, Chairs; Michael Shifter, Project Director
Independent Task Force Report No. 29 (2000)
Cosponsored with the Inter-American Dialogue

Future Directions for U.S. Economic Policy Toward Japan
Laura D'Andrea Tyson, Chair; M. Diana Helweg Newton, Project Director
Independent Task Force Report No. 28 (2000)

First Steps Toward a Constructive U.S. Policy in Colombia
Bob Graham and Brent Scowcroft, Chairs; Michael Shifter, Project Director
Interim Report (2000)
Cosponsored with the Inter-American Dialogue

Promoting Sustainable Economies in the Balkans
Steven Rattner, Chair; Michael B.G. Froman, Project Director
Independent Task Force Report No. 27 (2000)

Non-Lethal Technologies: Progress and Prospects
Richard L. Garwin, Chair; W. Montague Winfield, Project Director
Independent Task Force Report No. 26 (1999)

Safeguarding Prosperity in a Global Financial System: The Future International Financial Architecture
Carla A. Hills and Peter G. Peterson, Chairs; Morris Goldstein, Project Director
Independent Task Force Report No. 25 (1999)
Cosponsored with the International Institute for Economics

U.S. Policy Toward North Korea: Next Steps
Morton I. Abramowitz and James T. Laney, Chairs; Michael J. Green, Project Director
Independent Task Force Report No. 24 (1999)

Reconstructing the Balkans
Morton I. Abramowitz and Albert Fishlow, Chairs; Charles A. Kupchan, Project Director
Independent Task Force Report No. 23 (Web-only release, 1999)

Strengthening Palestinian Public Institutions
Michel Rocard, Chair; Henry Siegman, Project Director; Yezid Sayigh and Khalil Shikaki, Principal Authors
Independent Task Force Report No. 22 (1999)

U.S. Policy Toward Northeastern Europe
Zbigniew Brzezinski, Chair; F. Stephen Larrabee, Project Director
Independent Task Force Report No. 21 (1999)

The Future of Transatlantic Relations
Robert D. Blackwill, Chair and Project Director
Independent Task Force Report No. 20 (1999)

U.S.-Cuban Relations in the 21st Century
Bernard W. Aronson and William D. Rogers, Chairs; Walter Russell Mead, Project Director
Independent Task Force Report No. 19 (1999)

After the Tests: U.S. Policy Toward India and Pakistan
Richard N. Haass and Morton H. Halperin, Chairs
Independent Task Force Report No. 18 (1998)
Cosponsored with the Brookings Institution

Managing Change on the Korean Peninsula
Morton I. Abramowitz and James T. Laney, Chairs; Michael J. Green, Project Director
Independent Task Force Report No. 17 (1998)

Promoting U.S. Economic Relations with Africa
Peggy Dulany and Frank Savage, Chairs; Salih Booker, Project Director
Independent Task Force Report No. 16 (1998)

U.S. Middle East Policy and the Peace Process
Henry Siegman, Project Coordinator
Independent Task Force Report No. 15 (1997)

Differentiated Containment: U.S. Policy Toward Iran and Iraq
Zbigniew Brzezinski and Brent Scowcroft, Chairs; Richard W. Murphy, Project Director
Independent Task Force Report No. 14 (1997)

Russia, Its Neighbors, and an Enlarging NATO
Richard G. Lugar, Chair; Victoria Nuland, Project Director
Independent Task Force Report No. 13 (1997)

Rethinking International Drug Control: New Directions for U.S. Policy
Mathea Falco, Chair
Independent Task Force Report No. 12 (1997)

Financing America's Leadership: Protecting American Interests and Promoting American Values
Mickey Edwards and Stephen J. Solarz, Chairs; Morton H. Halperin, Lawrence J. Korb, and Richard M. Moose, Project Directors
Independent Task Force Report No. 11 (1997)
Cosponsored with the Brookings Institution

A New U.S. Policy Toward India and Pakistan
Richard N. Haass, Chair; Gideon Rose, Project Director
Independent Task Force Report No. 10 (1997)

Arms Control and the U.S.-Russian Relationship
Robert D. Blackwill, Chair and Author; Keith W. Dayton, Project Director
Independent Task Force Report No. 9 (1996)
Cosponsored with the Nixon Center for Peace and Freedom

American National Interest and the United Nations
George Soros, Chair
Independent Task Force Report No. 8 (1996)

Making Intelligence Smarter: The Future of U.S. Intelligence
Maurice R. Greenberg, Chair; Richard N. Haass, Project Director
Independent Task Force Report No. 7 (1996)

Lessons of the Mexican Peso Crisis
John C. Whitehead, Chair; Marie-Josée Kravis, Project Director
Independent Task Force Report No. 6 (1996)

Managing the Taiwan Issue: Key Is Better U.S. Relations with China
Stephen Friedman, Chair; Elizabeth Economy, Project Director
Independent Task Force Report No. 5 (1995)

Non-Lethal Technologies: Military Options and Implications
Malcolm H. Wiener, Chair
Independent Task Force Report No. 4 (1995)

Should NATO Expand?
Harold Brown, Chair; Charles A. Kupchan, Project Director
Independent Task Force Report No. 3 (1995)

Success or Sellout? The U.S.-North Korean Nuclear Accord
Kyung Won Kim and Nicholas Platt, Chairs; Richard N. Haass, Project Director
Independent Task Force Report No. 2 (1995)
Cosponsored with the Seoul Forum for International Affairs

Nuclear Proliferation: Confronting the New Challenges
Stephen J. Hadley, Chair; Mitchell B. Reiss, Project Director
Independent Task Force Report No. 1 (1995)

Note: Task Force reports are available for download from CFR's website, www.cfr.org.
For more information, email publications@cfr.org.

Made in the USA
Lexington, KY
20 January 2018